Fear of the Abyss

Fear of the Abyss

Healing the Wounds of Shame and Perfectionism

Aleta Edwards, Psy.D.

Red Pill Press
2016

Red Pill Press
An Imprint of Quantum Future Group
295 Scratch Branch Rd.
Otto, NC 28763
redpillpress.com

Contents

Dedication

I would like to dedicate this book to my husband, Rand, without whose support and sacrifice I could not have written this book. His support, his editorial comments, his multiple readings of the manuscript, and his handling of all the technical work were indispensable, but his emotional help and his belief in me and in the book were the greatest contributions of all.

Preface to the Second Paperback Edition

Since self-publishing the paperback edition of *Fear of the Abyss*, I have continued to receive numerous emails from readers sharing their lives with me and telling me how much the book has helped them. I love hearing from people. I have learned how very widespread the problem of shame really is. Telling people they do not have to be perfect does not address why they feel the need to be in the first place, and the underlying emotional wounds must be addressed for this to change. When people really change on a deep level, their dreams change and they catch themselves with surprise when they start to feel and respond differently to things that would have caused perfectionistic anxiety. This is very different from trying to talk yourself out of a feeling; instead, it is being pleasantly surprised as you catch these changes. It shows real change on an underlying level. I believe that we all have a need, whether or not we are aware of it, to be understood the way we really are, and this is my goal. I am gratified to have heard from so many wonderful people and hope that my book continues to help others. I'm happy and grateful that Red Pill Press has published my book, as it will be able to reach more people.

Dr. Aleta Edwards
Tampa, Florida
March 22, 2016

Preface to the First Paperback Edition

Since publishing the ebook version of *Fear of the Abyss* I have received hundreds of comments from readers, sharing their life stories and telling me how my book has helped them. I am very touched and gratified by their remarks and appreciate every one of them. Many have also encouraged me to publish a physical version of my book, and the book you are reading now is a response to these requests.

Dr. Aleta Edwards
Tampa, Florida
October 31, 2013

Preface

Why This Book?

In my years of practice as a psychologist, I have come to know that people can actually *heal*, not just cope better. While coping is important and helps get us through hard times, it is not the same as healing. Depending on the difficulty of their problems and the degree of self-examination they are willing to do, people can truly heal – leaving behind old patterns of behavior, as well as their attendant thoughts and feelings.

My orientation is psychodynamic, meaning that I believe in helping people get to the root of the issues that trouble them. A person's history or narrative, and the unconscious (thoughts and feelings not in awareness) are keys to this process. My goal in this kind of therapy is integration – to view the many different components of one's personality with love, compassion, and honor, and to understand that we all have some tendencies we don't like that can be tempered by the positive ones. It is unnecessary to deny these tendencies, which can leave people feeling inauthentic. What some call the shadow side must be acknowledged and embraced, not split off almost like a separate person. This book will not tell you how to cope with these feelings, but will encourage you to see yourself as a whole person – though maybe one with some feelings you have been running from – and set you on the path to healing.

Many people have come to realize the importance of awareness, of being in the present, of knowing who they really are. The way to do this is to see who you are *not*, to go through issues and defenses that obscure your real feelings. The rewards are great: healing from emotional wounds and much greater awareness. Unfortunately, many people who think of themselves as spiritual believe that they shouldn't have "negative" feelings. This is not true; the human being goes through many dark and difficult thoughts to arrive at true compassion or forgiveness, and this is definitely the case with self-awareness. To really know who you are, your core self, you need to know who you are pretending to be and who you are not, and the way to heal is the same way to grow in awareness.

I wrote this book to help those with a certain set of traits that I frequently see in my clients. Specifically, I have written this book for people who have problems with perfectionism, control issues, shame, problems making decisions, black-and-white thinking, a dread of criticism, poor self-esteem, a fear of being disappointed or disappointing others, an inhibited fantasy life, and problems with relationships that relate to these traits. I call this set of traits the *PCS constellation*, for Perfectionism, Control, and Shame. These issues are all interrelated and describe a certain *type* of person; they also cut across diagnostic lines. Although they may or may not have led to a formal diagnosis, they nonetheless present problems in living and feelings of unease.

Perfectionism is often the most obvious of the traits in this constellation or personality type. I believe that people with perfectionistic personalities actually feel anything *but* perfect. Maybe this describes *you*. Perhaps you, too, feel there is a horrible person hiding inside that you must always defend against. As one extremely bright and insightful young client put it, "Do you think I *like* being so rigid, strict, and judgmental? I *hate* it, but I'm afraid if I ever take one drink or go to one bar, I will be just like my parents. ... If I tell one lie or condone one little lie in someone else, I will become this horrible liar like they are, making excuses for things and never doing anything."

Those who feel this way do not yet know the tremendous healing power of processing their feelings and experiences. This processing does not happen quickly, and takes much hard work and at times painfully honest self-examination, but it is the only way to heal the emotional wounds that cause the troubling symptoms in the first place. While arduous, this path leads to tremendous rewards. It results in a more contented and calm person, one possessing more insight and depth and better able to develop authentic goals and carry them to completion. It leads to the realization that you have far more choices than you ever imagined, because you have decided to live with awareness. People are surprised and comforted to discover that telling their stories and exploring their feelings, while someone listens intelligently and compassionately, constitute a powerful healing tool.

While this book is not psychotherapy and cannot take its place, it does invite you to move toward self-awareness – to see yourself not as a label or problem, but as a rich and unique person with many productive, unproductive, and neutral traits. You can use this book alone, share it with a therapist, or use it in conjunction with a meditative practice.

My Hope

I hope you also *enjoy* this book. As you read parts of it that call on your honesty, strength, and courage, remember that people with these symptoms are usually very kind, moral, and ethical people. These are not traits you would or should ever want to change. Many people facing their own unique challenges in life struggle just to develop *some* of the fine qualities that come naturally to the PCS personality.

Remember that we are all "package deals." Our positive and negative traits come from the same place, and the life challenge is to bring more balance and awareness to our personalities. One client, a kind and loyal friend to those she knew, said that she wished she could be "witty and bubbly" like a friend of hers. This friend was good-hearted and nice, but not very stable or dependable. I told my client that, though she didn't "do witty and bubbly," she was an outstanding friend and person, and that the more spontaneous friend had to struggle against the flip side of her spontaneity, impulsivity.

The PCS person often judges herself in this way: she compares herself to those with qualities more valued in our culture, which too often underrates the more mature traits of dependability and compassion found in the PCS personality. Their sense of morality and concern about the way they affect others is often what brings them to therapy in the first place. So remember as you face your challenges that you are a good person trying to grow. As you expand your mind and realize how much strength and courage you are using, those too will become a genuine part of your self-image.

Introduction

I have written this book for a specific *type* of person, one that I frequently see in my private practice. These people – whom I refer to as "PCS personalities" – suffer from problems with perfectionism, control, and shame, but they also have trouble with making decisions, think in rigid black-and-white terms, live in dread of criticism (especially self-criticism), and experience poor self-esteem, among other characteristics. I like to picture the individual issues of this PCS constellation as the spokes of a wheel. The hub of this wheel is what PCS personalities really feel inside that drives them to have these problems. It is the center of this wheel that needs to heal; then the whole constellation of issues or symptoms can disappear.

Although the name "PCS personality" comes from just three of the traits often found in this personality – perfectionism, control, and shame – I could just as easily have chosen any of the others. PCS is simply a shorthand way to refer to all the traits which are all found to a degree in anyone with this personality. You might recognize some of these traits as those of Obsessive-Compulsive Disorder (OCD), but the clients I see with this personality type do not have the essential features of this disorder. People with true OCD, with their repetitive, often elaborate rituals, are in such pain that it often prevents them from participating in insight-oriented psychotherapy or even the type of self-reflection that is required by this book.

Thus, though the PCS personality may share some traits with the obsessive-compulsive, most come to me suffering from depression, anxiety, or panic disorders. Sometimes they have already been to another therapist who has told them that their anxiety or other symptoms are best treated with cognitive-behavioral therapy, which teaches coping devices to alleviate and control the symptoms. They learn these techniques but then are dissatisfied with the results, because they *know* on some level that something is causing them to have the symptoms that they continue to cope with. The symptoms that are being treated are merely the manifestation of their underlying feelings, which remain in place even after being taught new ways of "coping." No one has ever told them that there is hope that they can actually heal, by addressing the "hub" of their personality, the underlying dynamics that cause them to suffer. They have never been asked to tell their "story," the narrative of their lives that led to the symptoms. One very insightful young client told me in the first session that he felt like he had lost a part of himself and wanted to get it back. He was exactly right.

Although this book discusses some of the issues that trouble the PCS person in its individual chapters, it is not written for a specific problem – the "spokes" of the PCS wheel – but for a certain *type* of person who has these problems. There are numerous books available on anxiety, panic, or depression, but this book is for a certain *type* of person who may suffer from these. It is also not about coping, but rather about engaging in a truly healing process, a process that leads to greater awareness. This process is not an easy one. Those who enter therapy of any kind expecting a miracle that will transform their personalities overnight are hoping for the impossible. And, after all, who would really want our personalities to be so malleable that we might wake up one morning and not recognize ourselves? No, true change and healing take real work, the work of sometimes rigorous self-reflection and honesty, whether with the guidance of a professional psychotherapist or on your own.

Organization of the Book

Because the traits in the PCS constellation are so closely related, it is difficult to disentangle them and discuss them as individual issues. The linear structure of a book requires that I do this; however, the relatedness of the issues also requires that the reader always keep in mind how each trait is interconnected in the overall pattern of this personality. Within the book you will see that many chapters deal with individual "spokes" in the PCS Constellation, but that there is quite a bit of overlap among them because the issues have the same hub or root. Despite the repetition, the reader must still frequently return to chapters already read to gradually build up the big picture.

Given the need for a linear organization, here's how the book is laid out: Chapter One gives an overview of the constellation of PCS issues and discusses my objections to diagnostic labels. Chapters Two through Four discuss individual issues, or individual spokes – specifically, shame, rigidity, and disappointment. Chapter Five takes a break from individual issues to talk about two theories that explain how we develop these issues, because to increase your understanding of the constellation you need to know how development occurs. Chapters Six through Nine discuss the rest of the issues I have chosen to focus on in this book – control, decisions, fantasy, and relationship difficulties.

Chapter Ten focuses on the Abyss. While you can get tremendous relief from going beneath the surface issues to the part of the unconscious that is closer to your awareness, facing the Abyss is the hardest part of all, because it is usually furthest from our conscious awareness. In this chapter you'll find more advanced work that invites you to really look at what you are afraid of – the kind of person you fear you are under these specific traits. Chapter Eleven discusses Your Authentic Self, and the freedom and peace that come from having an integrated Self. When you can truly face the Abyss, the defenses against knowing your Authentic Self drop away, and you will never be the same.

The chapters on individual spokes contain exercises designed to help you gradually go deeper and deeper in knowing yourself. The beginning exercises help you to get comfortable with just having issues – as we all do – and to observe yourself without judgment. While many exercises focus on looking behind or beneath the issues, they also gradually invite you to get closer and closer to your real, Authentic Self. Change is difficult, and you'll need to muster up all your courage to do this work.

While these exercises may at times reduce you to tears, I invite you also to laugh! It can be tremendously liberating to laugh at ourselves, and it is a very natural reaction to discovering that the hidden "monster" inside of you is perhaps no more frightening than a small, cornered animal. In being "caught," the worst is over, as the fear is brought into the light.

You cannot expect to do an exercise once and reap the benefits of deep change. Therefore, I suggest that you keep a journal, and make the exercises part of your life until they become a part of you. As you go through this process you will get closer and closer to your unconscious, which means that you will know yourself better, and won't feel at the mercy of a mind you sometimes feel doesn't even belong to you. Greater self-awareness leads to greater control over yourself and your life. Keep repeating the exercises from each chapter until you do not need them. Each chapter has new ones, but the older ones need to become a part of you and your life as well.

My Clients

In my years as a clinician, I have enjoyed an extremely diverse practice. I have worked with men and women, gay and straight people, and people of different races, ages, and cultural-ethnic groups. I have done psychological evaluations with children, have done therapy with seniors in nursing homes, treated active-duty military, and have worked with private clients from many different groups. The PCS issues are not limited to any specific group, which makes them universal and very important to address.

Please note that while the people whose material inspired my vignettes all gave me permission to use their stories, the people you will meet in this book are composites. I changed gender, age, and circumstances, but the issues remain true to the ideas. Therefore, if you ever met anyone who inspired a vignette, you would not know it. At the same time, you may "see" yourself and many you know, because these issues are so prevalent, but any resemblance to actual people is simply a coincidence.

I do not know you personally, but would like to help you in your healing process. In my eighteen years of private practice, I have walked this path with many clients, and I have seen a great many people with these dynamics heal. There is no greater pleasure than when a client says to me, "Remember when I used to beat myself up over every little thing?" and then to savor how free she feels now. It has been my honor and privilege to help them on the path they walked with courage, honesty, and true desire for greater self-awareness.

The desire to not be afraid of hidden, cut-off parts of our minds, but to confront, own and, yes, make room for the so-called negativity is something we must all struggle with and, in my view, are meant to.

Healing does not mean never being sad. It means not being blinded by anxiety that seems to come from nowhere, always feeling you must tread water simply to avoid life's blows. Since you are reading this book, I know you want to begin the healing process, and I wish you the best in your journey.

Chapter 1

The PCS Constellation

The acronym PCS – for perfectionism, control, and shame – stands for the type of person this book is intended for. However, these are only three of the traits in this personality type, and others discussed throughout this book could equally well have been chosen to stand for the whole. We humans are made up of constellations of traits. When we have certain traits, we are very likely to have other corresponding traits that tend to go together.

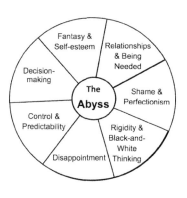

You are already familiar with constellations. You may have met people like my grandfather's neighbor, whom he used to call an "I can do you one better person." If someone didn't feel well, she would reply that she had bigger problems herself. If someone was proud of a grandchild, hers was better. Predictably she would become very angry if she thought someone else was bragging. Also very predictably, she would get depressed when people could not feed her desire for attention. You may also be familiar with people who are quick and funny, but know that they are often not dependable and can't plan well. You can see how certain traits go together – both the positive and negative aspects of whole personality types.

We all come as "packages" and our traits all have a positive side and a negative one. This is true not just of you, but of all of us. For example, people viewed as "control freaks" – and yes, they usually are PCS personalities – are wonderfully loyal, organized, and dependable. These traits are worth keeping, and the world badly needs them – but minus the terrible feelings of anxiety and self-doubt that can afflict someone with PCS issues. I am writing here for those who suffer from the more negative side of these traits, who work very hard and may be very accomplished, yet still cannot find peace or joy within themselves.

Do you suffer from anxiety that is coming from within, anxiety that seems unrelated to what is going on in your life? Do you feel that if you are not perfect in all that you do – that if you make just one mistake – you are no good? Do you have such a desire to be needed that you forget to need? Do you crave validation but have little self-love? Is it hard for you to admire someone or another person's talent without an unfavorable comparison to yourself? Do you overwork on the job and then feel unappreciated? Do you feel a need to make things predictable by trying to control them? Do you find it difficult to trust your intuitions about others, and second guess yourself, especially if you see or feel something negative? Do you find it hard to make decisions, as if each one were crucial? Is your thinking rigid? Do you have a dread of disappointment – either disappointing others or being disappointed?

If you answered "yes" to even a few of these questions, then you know the terrible discomfort that the PCS traits can bring. People have come to me for help with panic disorders, unaware of the connection to the PCS issues that set off the panic, and feeling as if it comes out of nowhere. Yet the human mind is exceedingly rich, with a logic all its own. The reasons for these attacks become clear only if we ask people to tell their stories, listen to them, and encourage them to listen to themselves. Some people come to therapy complaining of perfectionism and severe anxiety, and some of them tell me that they have in fact had full-blown obsessive-compulsive episodes, trapped in a hell of rituals that feel never-ending. They somehow moved beyond this, but suffer still, as the same personality remained.

While I am all in favor of coping – life certainly requires it – I feel very badly when people come to me who have been diagnosed with panic disorder and still suffer tremendously from their PCS issues *and* the panic attacks. While helping people manage their problems is important and useful, the problems, the real feelings underneath, go unaddressed. For example, people may have panic attacks because a part of the PCS constellation – the way they would *like* to think of themselves or others – is threatened by their real feelings about themselves or other coming into awareness. This person is very different from one suffering from panic due to, say, fear of abandonment. The same thing is true for depression. Is someone depressed because the need to believe oneself perfect (a PCS issue) is disrupted or is it due to some other reason?

Therefore, regardless of the surface diagnosis or the way symptoms manifest, I look both at the surface traits – the spokes of the wheel – and at the center, the actual hurt. This "hurt" is a kind of emotional unease that never really lets up, although with intense effort and defensive maneuvers it can be held at bay. To me that is like treading water: yes, staying alive and afloat is pretty important, but it would be nice to go somewhere. I feel sad when people come to me for the first visit and tell me what their diagnosis is, then make it apparent that their dynamics have never been addressed. What has really happened is that a very fragile defensive system had to face circumstances that caused its collapse. Much more can be done for someone than to help him get back to how he was before the crisis: the issues that made him vulnerable in the first place can be addressed.

The diagnostic labels people are given can obscure the actual personality core that causes the symptom or leads to the label. Likewise, looking at individual problems in isolation without an understanding of the *type* of person who has the problems can also hide what needs to heal. Before discussing the PCS constellation of traits more extensively below, let us take a closer look at some of the problems with applying diagnostic labels or looking at individual issues in isolation.

People vs. Labels

Nowadays, people often diagnose themselves before deciding to see a mental health professional. They will call me and declare that they have a panic or anxiety disorder, or are depressed. They are usually right. The problem is that the labels we give people, or which they may even give themselves, may prevent them from receiving the most effective treatment and achieving their optimum mental health and happiness. Focusing only on a label devalues the person and erases his or her personality. We all know that a person is not his symptoms or labels, but a whole human being. This whole person has a unique history, experience, and personality.

To a therapist who uses a psychoanalytic or holistic approach, these
labels are not nearly as important as *who* is suffering from the symptoms, the flesh-and-blood person who comes to us for help, and the
history that led them to our door. Each person's narrative is important and needs to be heard and honored. Perhaps the most important
idea in this book is that you are *not* your diagnosis, but a richly emotional human being with a story, layers of emotions, and interlocking
dynamics. Being treated accordingly, and learning to treat yourself
accordingly, is a huge step toward healing.

Let's look at some examples of how clients with the same diagnosis
might have very different problems, which require different approaches.
This will also help us home in on exactly who this book is intended for.
Many of the clients I see complain of feeling depressed. Imagine two
people becoming very depressed after being fired from a job. The first
person lacks needed job skills and feels too overwhelmed and worried
to even look for a new job. The second person is highly-skilled and
in a good position to find another job, but feels stupid, believing that
bright people don't get fired from their jobs. The second person is a
PCS type, because shame and wounded pride are at the core of his
depression. His perfectionism suffered a severe blow. The first faces
straightforward issues of loss and concern about the future, and has an
entirely different personality type.

Similarly, a person might be clinically depressed after the breakup
of a relationship because of grief and missing the person terribly, while
another is depressed because being rejected caused intense feelings of
shame, feelings so strong the person cannot even get to the point of
missing the one who was lost. The first person suffers from normal
feelings of loss, while the second suffers from wounded pride and shame,
and perhaps feelings of failure, which are issues of the PCS personality
type. Consider one more case: One person had a terrible childhood and
has never been able to enjoy life no matter what, because the base for
a happy life just wasn't there. She is always lethargic and has little
interest in anything. Another is thrown into emotional crisis because
of failing a subject in school – not because she couldn't stay in school,
but because she felt she failed. We have again the same diagnosis –
depression – but in very different types of people. The second person
is the PCS type: the perfectionist could not handle failing a test.

Anxiety is another common complaint that cannot be understood without knowing the personality type and underlying dynamics of the person having the symptom. For instance, someone may develop an anxiety disorder after a divorce due to a fear of doing things alone, while someone else in the same situation might have a dread of being criticized when trying new things. Again, the second person has the PCS personality; a dread of criticism is at the core of the anxiety.

In each of these illustrations the two people share a diagnosis, but you can see that their underlying issues are very different, and I would never treat their problems the same way.

A more extreme example of why we cannot just look at symptoms but must look at the person who has them, occurred in my practice several years ago. "Debbie" had had a very deprived and painful childhood. To survive it, she developed a PCS type of personality, which provided her with rules to give order to her chaotic world. As an adult she was quite rigid and anxious. Because she was usually depressed, yet managed to pull her mood up to normal from time to time, she described herself as having "mood swings." When Debbie went to a psychiatrist and told him about her "mood swings," she was diagnosed with Bipolar Disorder, a serious psychological condition for which she was given heavy-duty medication. The only problem was that she was never bipolar! In our sessions we dealt with the deep shame she felt about herself and the painful childhood that caused her many symptoms. In the course of her treatment there was no evidence of Bipolar Disorder, and her medication was stopped early on.

It is the perfectionism, dread of criticism, and shame of the PCS people in each of these examples that lie at the root of their problems, after life circumstances prevented their normal defenses from working. The other people in the examples do *not* have the same issues, but would be given the same diagnostic label. Treating depression, anxiety, or any other symptom without considering *who* has it will not allow anyone to really heal. It does people a huge disservice, and does not promote change – it just sends people back to whatever defended state they were in before the emotional crisis occurred.

I have seen so many people who have suffered greatly treated in this way when their perfectionism or some other PCS issue was challenged, and their real issues had never been touched. Whether you work on issues yourself or go to a psychotherapist, know your issues so you can get help for them. Your issue is never depression or anxiety. That is simply a diagnostic label. You could say that the depression or the anxiety is the *result* of the issues you have been living with all your life.

The Panic Disorder diagnosis is another in which aspects of the PCS constellation often play a role, and where it is essential to look beneath the label to see the real person. There are certainly people who have always been nervous and fearful, who have occasional panic attacks, and who are *not* PCS personalities. But the PCS issues are the first suspect when a new client reports having panic attacks. When I meet such a person, the first thing I ask myself is: Why did he develop the panic *now*? When years have gone by, we need to know why and when the panic attacks developed, and what was going on at the time.

"Lois" came to me complaining of panic attacks. She suffered from agoraphobia, which sometimes prevented her from leaving home, and laughingly told me that she had "a messed up brain." I asked her when these problems began and what was happening at that time. If she was not always like this, why did she think that she had something wrong with her brain? Something must have transpired to cause her to develop the panic in the first place. Lois replied that the panic began when she divorced her physically-abusive husband and moved into her own place a few years earlier. He still came around and wanted her to go places with him. She was afraid to turn him down, and felt guilty that she had divorced him. She developed agoraphobia, which gave her a reason to not have to go with him, and he would then respond by calling her "crazy."

I asked Lois if she had been abused as a child and she told me a very sad story of how she had been afraid walking home from school, because her father, waiting for her and her siblings to arrive, would physically abuse them. She described incredibly scary and violent scenes. Over the course of many sessions, it became clear that to survive a horrendous childhood, Lois developed a PCS personality. She gave order to a piece of her world as best a small child could. She was "supposed" to love her mother and father. Later, she was "supposed" to love her husband. These "*supposed tos*" reflect rigid, black-and-white thinking, a component of the PCS personality. No extenuating circumstances are permitted: one is just "supposed to" do or feel certain things all the time. Because she needed to develop a system to survive a terrible childhood, Lois never processed her feelings for her father, never questioned her love for this brutal man.

One day Lois went to the bathroom during our session. She returned crying, but smiling – yes, both at once – and said, "I get it! I don't have to love anyone I don't want to! My father was a crazy, violent bastard and I married someone just like him – and I hate him, too!" To a large extent, her panic disorder and agoraphobia disappeared from that day forward. We discussed how being sad is so much easier than being panicked, and how blaming herself for not doing the impossible had seemed better than facing the severe damage done to her. Lois did not have a defective brain. She was not unhelpable. But she *did* have to address the rigidity of her black-and-white thinking to truly heal.

When I first met Lois, she had been on medication for three years. She had been told that there is no cure for panic disorder and was sent to classes in relaxation. They helped the panic somewhat but didn't get rid of it, which is why she had sought me out. Lois knew on some level she had not really touched the problem. A few days after our initial session, I received a letter from her psychiatrist saying that she had a severe panic disorder and was a dependent person, and that I needed to do some cognitive-behavioral work with her – the same coping work she had already done. But with Lois's hard work and insight, and without any more "coping" techniques, her panic disorder was finally cured. The medication was no longer necessary. She was able to tell her former husband that she wanted nothing to do with him and that she was living her own life.

Lois lost years of her life because the system had labeled her and turned her into another "incurable" person whose only recourse was to learn to cope. No one had asked her when or why she had developed her problems, how she had lived before that, or looked at her strengths as well as her overall personality. No one had looked at her at all as a whole person – just at the panic disorder.

In the case of anxiety and panic disorders, I think it is especially critical to address the issues underlying them. They *are* curable. I have personally seen these symptoms healed in a great many people, and I wish the same for everyone. Again, the symptoms are but a manifestation of the underlying feelings that develop into a total personality. Treating these symptoms means ignoring the personality and devaluing the person. The symptoms are not the point – they are just the most noticeable things.

With Lois, this process took about eight months. She did not want to delve very deeply into why she developed this defense. Some of my clients, like Lois, want only symptomatic relief, while others want to maximize their self-awareness for its own sake. She said that she was getting older and just wanted to live, which made sense to me. She came to my office about a year later to tell me she had gotten a terrific job in a field she cared deeply about. She was using her creative talents and enjoying it tremendously. Like many others with her issues, Lois had siblings with similar ones, and she went on to be a source of significant help to them.

Now that I have shown how different people with the same presenting symptoms may have a very different path to these symptoms, I want to briefly discuss what I mean by "dynamics." This is the key to understanding the PCS constellation, which will be discussed later.

What Are "Dynamics?"

Why do I combine a variety of diagnostic categories into the same constellation of PCS traits, and what do these traits have in common? They all stem from the same underlying "dynamics." Dynamics refers to how our unconscious thoughts and feelings make us consciously feel and then act in certain ways.

The idea that we are driven by unconscious factors is certainly not new. Freud is famous for developing the idea that we have an unconscious mind, things we are not aware of, things we hide from ourselves. Certainly we have all seen people we have said are "in denial," an example of what Freud had in mind. If a life event triggers a feeling we have secretly or unconsciously had all along, an emotional crisis can occur. Again, think of Lois. I did not see a panic disorder, but a frightened woman who felt she was "supposed to" love an abusive father, and who attempted to ease her guilt by trying to love an abusive husband. She was trying to beat herself into submission, just as she had been taught to do. PCS people "play by the rules," but have often not been taught a rule for self-preservation or happiness.

Psychotherapists with a psychoanalytic orientation have great respect for the unconscious and its dynamics. However, our culture has gotten carried away with labels, which then often determine the type of treatment we receive. These labels ignore dynamic factors, especially the underlying unconscious feelings that affect each person's experiences and are, in turn, affected *by* them. We can feel trapped by these feelings and are freed only when they are under our conscious control.

Recall my earlier examples. One person lost a job and became depressed because he lacked skills and worried about eventual homelessness, and another was depressed because he felt stupid. Someone can be depressed either because of unbearable loneliness and grief, or because of shame and a fear of facing his own feelings. These are not the same kinds of people. Although both suffer from depression, they have very different *dynamics*. This is yet another reason why I de-emphasize diagnostic labels in my work. I have seen too many people suffer for too long because their narrative and dynamics went ignored.

The anxiety you feel doesn't just come out of nowhere: it arises because a delicate defensive system is being threatened. Picture a thought as a physical form and your defenses as a metal censor that you put between your thoughts and your conscious awareness. Now picture the thought banging itself against that censor over and over. Every time that happens the clash causes panic or anxiety. Your resistance to it causes pain. If you can lower that resistance or take down the barrier you will not compound the pain of the thought itself. In fact, without the resistance you will only have the thought or feeling, although it is likely to be a sad one or you wouldn't have erected the barrier in the first place.

For example, people who are extremely perfectionistic and anxious about it really don't feel perfect at all. They usually feel quite badly about themselves and try to prevent others from seeing any vulnerability; they even avoid seeing any themselves, in order to push back painful and negative feelings. We all have negative feelings   a whole range of them – and when we do not acknowledge them, they keep trying to be heard. Here lies the source of anxiety. But when it happens it is nothing more than your own mind trying to get you to accept and acknowledge these feelings, not a disease or something that comes from elsewhere.

People get so tired keeping up this defensive facade. At some point, you need to see exactly what you don't like in yourself, whether or not it is fair, as often it is not, and this will relieve the anxiety of needing to be perfect. Why not give yourself the chance to really know yourself, to expand your self-awareness and become a whole person? Your anxiety is simply a part of yourself trying to get acknowledged, not an enemy. The better you know yourself, the more control you really have. You then do not have to worry about a part of your being that, contained by a barrier, could come bursting out, because it is under your conscious control. It is the pent-up people who tend to lose control, not those who are in touch with their feelings. Becoming aware of unconscious feelings will *not* take away your morality, spirituality, or ethics, but *will* take away the experience of feelings arising that seem to come from out of nowhere.

For your own well-being, I ask you to look at yourself with sincere and profound honesty, in order to face the sometimes painful feelings that lie beneath the surface. Maybe they won't be so bad when you examine them, and maybe you will come to see the goodness in yourself as you go through this book and the process it encourages. This is my hope. I constantly see just how hard people are on themselves; the irony is that, when they look further inward, intense emotional courage emerges. This, then, becomes a resource and a genuine part of their self-image.

The PCS Constellation

We have all met perfectionists. They're the ones who have to have everything "just right," even when a slight omission or error will hardly be noticed. Working with others, or being in a relationship, can present serious problems because perfectionists also feel compelled to prevent others from "messing up," since this will also reflect on them and disturb their tidy view of the way the world should be. This is how they get their reputations as "control freaks." What may be less obvious is that when a perfectionist does make that rare mistake, her underlying reaction is often one of shame. You will learn the reasons why later.

For now, let me just say that, for the perfectionist, it is *morally wrong* to make a mistake, so to make one means being *immoral* – a bad person. Shame and perfectionism often go together.

Do *you* feel devastated when you make a mistake? Do *you* then draw the conclusion that you are in some way completely unworthy or unacceptable? You, like many others, may dread humiliation and yet feel humiliated for common, run-of-the-mill mistakes. The shame you feel can lead you to deny your true feelings to both yourself and others.

Other traits belonging to the PCS constellation are black-and-white thinking and indecisiveness. There are few "gray areas" for the PCS person. A course of action is either right or wrong. There is no such thing as a "little white lie." It is easy to see where the PCS person's indecisiveness comes from when situations are all black or all white and so much rides on each decision. It is especially sad to see this kind of thinking in intelligent people, as most of my PCS clients have been, because it sacrifices the subtlety that one usually sees in the thinking of intelligent people.

"Jeff" was a young client who expressed a resigned sadness over losing friends because he always tells the truth. He explained that if someone asks him if he likes a new haircut, for example, he feels compelled to tell the truth, rather than soften the blow. He would do this regardless of how close he was to the person or the context. When I explained to him that there are levels of truth and sharing of opinions, he said to me, "I know that. I don't like being this way. I can't help it." To this otherwise highly intelligent man, telling a lie is one option and is bad, and bad people do it; telling the truth is the only other option and is good, and good people do that. If only life were that neat and simple!

But, of course, that is the longing of the PCS person. This far-above-average man engaged in highly simplistic reasoning, a sure clue to the therapist that this is an emotional and defensive maneuver. Jeff's comment that he couldn't help telling the exact truth was especially moving to me, as most PCS people would attempt to justify what they were doing; Jeff, in contrast, knew that something made him like this and he did not defend it, but owned it as his issue.

Another characteristic of PCS thinking is concreteness. In the past, when I did a lot of intelligence testing, I would often see PCS issues and anxieties. Using abstract reasoning and intuition are extremely anxiety-producing for PCS people, who would often lose points on one test in particular. To use an example similar to one on the test, when I asked a highly intelligent woman how a pot and a pan are alike, she immediately said both were used in cooking, a perfect response and correct abstraction. Then she looked panicked, and blurted out, "No! Don't count that! Both are made of metal!" She took a perfect, 2-point response and completely ruined it, getting no points at all. The generalization was too uncomfortable for the tighter, smaller world with which she is more comfortable. Similarly, when you ask a PCS person how "left" and "right" are alike, they will often look at you with evident discomfort and say that they are in fact opposites. The idea of opposites having something in common is clearly too uncomfortable for people who engage in rigid, black-and-white thinking.

The PCS traits can affect every aspect of your life. For example, you may have a strong need to be needed, as this validates you and counteracts underlying feelings of not being worthy. Yet in a healthy relationship both parties should need and be needed. In a relationship everyone likes to contribute, to be valued, and to feel competent. If you are the type who is always giving, maybe you have noticed that your loved ones, whether friends or romantic partners, often seem un-appreciative – see you as too controlling or get annoyed with you. That is because your need to be needed overwhelms their need to feel competent, to make their own contribution, and your own need to need. In my experience PCS people are extremely kind and caring people. The problem is – and there will be more on this in the chapter on re-lationships – that this dynamic doesn't leave much room for the other person's goodness or kindness.

Chances are, if you are reading this book, that you are good at giving and not so good at letting people give to you. I once had a client (who was *not* a PCS type) who complained that his girlfriend was too perfect, taking charge of everything. She did such an excellent job, that he felt she didn't need him. He didn't understand that she did it in a desperate attempt to keep him around, to make him see her as good, and *she* didn't understand that he needed to feel good about himself, too. People don't really want someone perfect, but someone with whom they feel good about themselves. As you know, however, anxiety can drive you on, even when you see that what you are doing is causing harm to a relationship you value. Is your need to be perfect and to be needed preventing someone else from growing, contributing, and feeling like a valued equal?

On those occasions when I have had to cancel an appointment due to illness or an emergency, my PCS clients have always expressed a sincere concern for me and assured me that they would be fine. You, too, are no doubt a very caring and kind person, and no one would change that. Yet, as I have said, traits have positive and negative aspects; keeping the positive and not being tormented by the negative is what my approach is all about. The challenge is to achieve balance; while your giving nature is much appreciated, you need to let others give and to accept from them as well. The world needs ethical and compassionate people, but it is the self-torment of the PCS personality that needs to be healed, not the character. You can keep your wonderful traits yet stop beating up on yourself, and that is our goal.

There are also many people who are not PCS types who are rigid, neat freaks, or abusive. A lot of people have *some* PCS traits – they are, after all, very human issues – but they have problems with a self that fragments. A crucial thing you must remember and understand is that a PCS person is *not* just one whose personality happens to have some of the same traits, but one who is also an ethical person who cares about right and wrong, how others are treated, and who has excellent self-control. A PCS person does not and would not abuse. If you have serious problems with anger or violence, or you make poor choices that harm yourself and disregard others, then you are not a PCS person. While this book may give you insight into some issues, you do not have the kind of Abyss discussed in this book.

The Abyss

Why should PCS people be this way? I have found that, on a deeper level, people suffering from PCS dynamics have what I call a *fear of the Abyss*. They fear that should they let up on their rigid control, a very bad person, lurking within their dark side or Abyss, will be released and dominate their personality. What they often fear is that they will become like some person, usually a parent or other important person in their early lives, some of whose habits or personality they abhor and feel they have within themselves. It is no wonder people with PCS complain of poor self-esteem. Feeling you have some kind of monster inside will not make anyone feel good – quite the opposite.

My clients with PCS issues always have this Abyss, like the workaholic who is afraid of being lazy, or the person who must stick to the exact truth at all times, even at the risk of offending others, because he fears becoming a liar. This fear of the Abyss is rooted in the mistaken belief that one must hide from a part of oneself at any cost to keep the lid on. It is a waste of energy going through life defending against these painful and scary feelings. It is far better to confront the feelings and live fully.

I cannot describe to you the joy I have felt when clients who have faced their Abyss have told me how situations that in the past would have been extremely anxiety-producing and painful became more neutral, and were faced with calm. One client who had always striven to be at the top of her classes in college reported that she got a B on a test and that she got home and realized that she hadn't even tried to find out who got the As, that she didn't care, and that she wasn't depressed. She no longer feared the flawed, imperfect, but normal human being she truly was. Another client, a workaholic, told me her boss made yet one more unreasonable demand, and that she had told her she would be glad to do the task if the boss prioritized the other ones and gave her time...and that it was easy! She worried no more about being considered lazy, or considering herself lazy, if she didn't comply with her boss's every request.

These clients told me that the absence of guilt and shame in these situations was like a huge weight being removed from them. They did not work directly on saying no or not being perfect, but worked instead on the hurt underneath. They faced the Abyss. When people are able and willing to do this, the defenses against knowing themselves drop away, the sign of a real and true change.

Thus, what I am calling the Abyss is a belief about the Self, and the fears related to this belief that are not integrated and take inordinate amounts of energy to hold back. Jungians call this Abyss the "Shadow," and it is important to understand that it can be integrated and absorbed into your overall personality. What are you if you do not toe the line to keep proving you are not bad in some way?

People with this personality have very specific, if unconscious, ideas about the dreaded part of the Self they run from; the PCS traits keep that knowledge from the Self. Doing things to counteract those feelings of anxiety, panic and sadness when your real thoughts and feelings try to connect with you is the antithesis of true healing. Embracing the so-called negative feelings and making them part of the Whole You is the way to heal. When the positive and negative feelings are not split apart, but modulate each other, one reaches a mature acceptance of issues that still need work without feeling so terrible.

Life Lessons

I hold dear the belief that there is a very real connection between our minds, bodies, and spirits, and that there are life lessons we must all experience to gain wisdom and raise ourselves to a higher level of awareness. I do not mean to imply that we are here to be perfect, but I do believe we are here to progress further in awareness and actions, and advance beyond where we started when we came into the world. Life is like a school, and if we knew it all in the beginning there would be no point to being here. I see self-awareness as the link to spirituality because, ironically, focusing on ourselves and gaining understanding leads us to see that not everything is about us. We are then free to notice and enjoy some wonderful things about the world that we were not in touch with before.

I have known many people struggling with a particular life lesson in therapy, when suddenly a challenging situation presents itself that relates directly to this struggle, as if to say "Now it's time to deal with this once and for all." For example, one young client, whose mother favored his younger sister, had a job in which a promotion he felt should have been his was given to a very young woman who had just started. This reverberated in my client because of his family history. Another client who had a very high-paying job but always worried about money began to address the issue of how money represented love and security to him. About a week after he made this connection, he went on a business trip and had two hundred dollars stolen from him. I cannot tell you how many times something like this has happened, not where a person has set himself up, but where life has stepped in with his issue and almost screamed out, "Here is a life lesson for you!"

While alleviating suffering is the immediate goal of therapy, on the road to this we often search for why it occurred in the first place, what life lesson it is teaching. So, in addition to understanding our feelings, whether conscious or unconscious, and how they relate to our experiences, we must also come to know their *meaning*. This meaning places our past suffering into a larger context and provides comfort and guidance for us in the future. Seeing life as a journey has enabled me to have and to share hope with others.

Hope for Healing

Because of my many experiences with people like Lois, who have spent years learning to cope and being told there was no cure, I feel strongly that people with PCS issues need to have their dynamics addressed. These are human beings whose lives matter! You may say, "Yes, your point is well taken, but what about managing the panic until the person does address the underlying issues?" You would be right. It *does* need to be managed if it is severe, with coping techniques, perhaps with medication, or both. But that is not the end of it. Coping and drugs do not heal the wounds that caused the problem. We seem to have forgotten that healing is possible, and that it is not really so difficult to help bring issues to light and facilitate real healing.

If you have a panic or anxiety disorder, ask yourself when you started to have problems, where you were, what you were doing, and what caused it. Remember the time you didn't have panic and ask yourself what changed and what happened in your life to affect you so deeply. As with Lois, it is usually a guilt-producing thought or feeling that you avoid at all costs. When faced, it does not produce unbearable guilt and pain. When kept from awareness, the thought or feeling has infinite power to terrorize. As with many fears, it is the unknown that causes the greatest pain and suffering.

You may have some or all of the issues I address. The diagnostic labels can vary, as you have seen. Many of the issues faced by those with the PCS constellation are those covered in later chapters. Because so many people have been diagnosed with panic disorder, anxiety disorder, or depression who have these issues, it is most important to stress that we need to think of the *person* who has the diagnosis. It is not, for example, the depression that is important, but *who* is depressed and *why*. This is the psychodynamic or holistic view. Thus, does a person develop panic disorder because a life event threatened to bring down his whole line of defenses, to bring things to the surface he is unprepared for? Or is it a person who has always been extremely anxious? I am not saying that the second type is not helpable by any means, but I *am* saying that these are very, very different people, and that the common label can be misleading and *has* been misleading.

What if life suddenly forces a PCS person to deal with failure? The whole defensive system can collapse and we then have a very depressed PCS person. This is very different from a person who is depressed due to a loss or grief. When a disorder is caused by repressed and denied thoughts and feelings coming to light without the appropriate therapeutic work on them, it is not only possible to get help for the crisis state, but to have a stronger and more authentic structure than before. A depressed PCS person can overcome the need to feel perfect as well as overcome the depression. This is what we mean when we say that a crisis can be a gift, an opportunity for growth. People I have worked with have often said after they were better that they were glad they experienced a crisis, because they live better lives now after gaining more self-awareness.

Coping is very important in life and we all have a lot to cope with. However, coping is not the same as healing. One of my clients had always coped beautifully until she had a life crisis, and then she developed a panic disorder very quickly. This client had gone to college and received a degree selected by her parents. Like most PCS people, she dreaded disappointing anyone, so she went on and got a job in her parents' chosen field. She did well, but was miserable. She could not live out her parents' dreams anymore and pretend she was happy. She idealized her parents as part of her perfectionism and denied the problem in her relationship with them. She would panic every day going to work.

As soon as she acknowledged being unhappy in the career she did not choose, the panic was almost gone. The defenses had fallen apart. She was living out the dreams of her parents, pretending to be happy while she was not, and her whole system failed. While this was very painful, it was beneficial to her, as she healed the very feelings that made her dread disappointing her parents in the first place. She would not have been able to do this had her coping been working. Healing occurs when you face your underlying issues. This book encourages you to become more self-aware, to move into the healing process.

If you go into therapy for depression, panic, or anxiety and you have the PCS dynamics, make sure you go to a therapist who can work with you on your issues so that you can achieve your maximum healing. I have had many people call me, say they have obsessive-compulsive traits and an anxiety disorder, have done research, learned that there is no cure and that cognitive-behavioral therapy is the best. When I told them the kind of therapy I do, some decided to go elsewhere. Many of them returned, however, unsatisfied with the feelings they were left to "cope" with. I believe the human experience is too rich and subtle for all of it to be examined by empirical research. Life and the human mind hold many wonderful and abstract phenomena that do not lend themselves to exact measurement, such as the joy of relating to another person without making cruel comparisons with oneself.

I have seen people heal, over and over, and addressing dynamics and facing long-denied or repressed truths is very powerful. While I understand that you just want your anxiety to go away, it is very important to remember that it is not an outside entity and that you should listen to what it is trying to tell you. After all, it is just a part of you asking for acknowledgment and a place in your overall personality. You could even think of anxiety as a call to better mental health, because when you heed what it tells you, you won't need to be afraid of those thoughts and feelings surfacing any longer.

In Chapter Five we will look at why people have these issues and how people develop psychologically. Different PCS issues will be discussed in each chapter. There is no hierarchy to these issues, and please remember the analogy I made with a wheel and its hub and spokes. We will deal with the spokes, which no doubt do feel like a long list of problems to you, but really have one center. When that center is more in balance so are the spokes, or symptoms.

Exercise

In this book I am going to suggest a series of exercises that you can do starting with the one below, and which you can continue doing as you read each subsequent chapter, as they take a lot of work and do not result in an immediate change. This is good. I always tell my clients that it is good that change is hard. I know when I go to bed at night that I will not wake up a criminal, that I have a solid and real core. So do you. If you changed too quickly, there would be no process and you wouldn't grow – you would just be someone else – and I want you to have the benefit of your hard work. Try these exercises and you will find that you begin to stretch your mind, giving it more options and expanded awareness.

Make a list of the issues troubling you the most. Then list the dynamic, your likely behavior, and the consequence. The idea here is not to have an exhaustive list, but to begin the process of being comfortable with having issues and acknowledging this to yourself with compassion and respect. Just be aware of them. You are reading this book, so you have decided that you want greater self-awareness and understand it as part of the healing process. You cannot blame yourself for your feelings or how they came to be, but you can start looking at how your feelings affect your behavior, which in turn can keep you from progressing.

A sample list follows on the next page. This list may work for you or you may have a different one, but the point is to recognize that you are a person seeking healing and greater self-awareness, and you are increasing your comfort with looking at dynamics you would like to change. Try not to judge these. Everyone has them; it is just that you have taken a step away from denial.

Issue	Dynamic	Behavior	Consequence
Control and Predictability	I am afraid of the unknown	I over plan vacations	Arguments with spouse over no free time
Perfection and Shame	I am afraid of being criticized	I do too much	I am tired
Rigid Morality	I am afraid of being wrong in any way	I am staying in a relationship that is abusive because I promised this was forever	I am unhappy

Table 1

Chapter 2

Shame & Perfectionism

Sadly, just about everyone at some point or other has experienced humiliation. Shame hurts so much that we find it hard to even think about it, and we then dedicate intense effort to making sure it never happens again. Shame and embarrassing situations provide the basis for a lot of the comedies we watch, and we laugh out of sympathy for the character, feeling glad that the embarrassing event didn't happen to us. Everyone has gone

through something that for them was very painful and shame-inducing, and in my experience the best way to deal with shame is to face it, to take the dread and power out of the memory. It is not pleasant to do this, but the rewards are very great. Shame is a strange emotion; it thrives on secrecy, but when held up to the light tends to whither and die.

Many people with PCS personality traits have a deep sense of shame – so powerful that they can't even say why something would be so devastating to them. For many of us there have been painful times in life when our dignity was under attack, and it is crucial to face these memories in order to move on. Shame is, in fact, the terrible feeling we experience when our dignity is attacked and we believe it was taken from us. However, both my general life experience and experience as a psychologist have shown me that dignity is not something that can actually be taken from someone.

It is my strong belief that dignity is inherent and is our birthright. I have worked with people who have had terrible things done to them.

One thing I discovered many years ago is that, while you can certainly be hurt psychologically, your dignity remains intact. In all of my work with people who have sustained all kinds of abuse, I have seen the dignity emanating from them, and I realized that while the memories are excruciating, their dignity was not destroyed. Dignity is something that gives us an obligation and responsibility in how we treat ourselves and others. You may feel you have lost yours, or have been cut off from it, but it is there, as surely as your heartbeat is there. You have been given life, and you are meant to be here. No matter how afraid you feel or how much pain you have, you are *deserving* of respect, and that is dignity, regardless of how you have been treated. Understanding this is extremely important.

Cruelty makes people think that their dignity was robbed, but people can only attack their own dignity. People who hurt others usually feel out of touch with their own dignity and want to bring someone else down. For example, I have seen many clients who were sexually abused, which has horrible psychological effects. Yet, they must come to realize that, as terrible as it was, and with all the issues to be dealt with, they are not corrupted; the ugliness belongs to the perpetrator, not the one who was hurt. This is an important spiritual concept.

Having been shamed does not mean you are corrupted, but that you have been touched by someone who was. You deserve respect because you have dignity. The soul, being, essence, or whatever word you personally use, that lives in your body, is intact and *you* must start by recognizing and respecting that dignity every day. You can corrupt yourself or decide you don't want your dignity when you abuse others, but no one can *take* yours away. You are, in a very real sense, intact. This is the first thing you must realize when dealing with shame. It is our duty to respect the dignity of other living beings, but we are not the ones who give it or take it away. It is a gift of life to have a childhood in which one's dignity is respected – a gift too many parents don't know how to give – but parents cannot give you dignity because you were born with it. What remains is to understand that and to separate out very hurt feelings from a *true* loss of dignity.

A chapter on shame would not be complete without a word about bodily functions. Everyone has a body and all bodies have functions. We live in a society in which functions are hidden, and there are thousands of products to help us do that, yet everyone still has functions. When children are being toilet trained, some parents use shame to push them along, making the children feel dirty, disgusting, and, yes, ashamed. Some parents use shame around other issues, but I am asking you to look inside yourself and to realize that your dignity resides within and is intact. No matter how traumatized you may have been, no matter how psychologically hurt, you must now realize that *you*, the essence of you, your soul if you prefer – the real you – is intact.

I believe that doctors and nurses who work with very sick people already know this. They see the dignity in each person and realize that things can go wrong with the body, and yet the real person's dignity is intact. Whether due to an illness, an accident, or psychological or physical abuse, you must realize that whatever happened to you to make you feel shame could happen to anyone, and that while someone may have tried very hard to attack your dignity and might have made you feel very bad, your dignity is a birthright and was not given or taken away by them. You must realize that while one can be broken physically or psychologically, the essence or real person is intact.

I used to work in a nursing home doing therapy with the residents. I knew a woman who had been paralyzed for many years, but her mind was sharp and she was extremely well-informed. Not only was she bored lying in bed all the time, as she had no family or living friends to visit her, she also needed help with her personal routine in every way. There were painful times when a nurse or nurse's assistant would be rushed and be sharp with this proud woman. Yet, she told me that many times a day, she would try to elevate her thoughts, to remember that, while she lived in her body, she was not just her body, and that – invisible though she may be to some people, and unable to care for herself – she was a good and worthy human being. This woman suffered terribly, but she was in touch with her own dignity. In all her suffering, she did not suffer shame.

I once had a client who had been raped and beaten on her way home by a group of men; while this occurred, as if it weren't bad enough, the men said extremely cruel things to her, telling her she was ugly as they beat her and mangled her face. She had had several surgeries to make her face presentable once more. She came to therapy for post-traumatic stress, and she said that she wanted the flashbacks to stop and didn't want to be afraid to leave her house. She also told me, "I have heard of things like this happening and victims feeling ashamed. I am not ashamed. I have done nothing wrong."

While this client faced a long road ahead, she was aware that her dignity was intact. I have worked with people who have suffered all kinds of terrible experiences – and being made fun of can hurt just as much as physical abuse – and my first therapeutic task was *always* to help them understand that, while their minds and their bodies may hurt a great deal, the dignity of their essence was clean and intact. Dignity is always there and is supposed to be respected. When people don't respect yours, they are attacking their own by their own free will, but cannot attack yours. Whatever you have suffered, others have suffered as well, and you would never dream of viewing them as lacking dignity. The way to overcome shame is to face painful memories and keep a strong hold of your own dignity, invisible though it may be to you, but just as strong as anyone's.

When you remember things that caused you shame, you should not laugh, and you may in fact cry. Crying is honest, and you can begin to heal by giving yourself the message that you do not think your experience was funny. So many times clients have told me about something very cruel that was done to them, and they laugh. I do not laugh. They usually look at my face and begin to cry. They see that I can see their dignity, and when they look in the mirror that I often am for people, they can cry for the hurt because they realize they are worth crying for. Think of the dignity of a newborn, a puppy, a sick person, a very old person; no matter how you feel about someone, the living spark is in them and must be respected, and so must yours. This is what I mean by dignity.

I have said this over and over because it is so very important. There is nothing wrong with a sense of humor or gently laughing at oneself if it is not done with self-disdain. For example, as we discussed in the Introduction, it may feel natural to you to laugh as we uncover certain "deep dark secrets" that aren't so "dark" after all. However, I have known people who have always played the clown, refer to themselves as someone who "goofs up," and who say other cruel things about themselves. I believe that they are preempting an attack on their own dignity by doing this to themselves. When you have true respect and compassion for yourself, you can laugh at yourself and at the frailty of human beings in general, and this is a positive gesture – but until you are at this point it is better to work on connecting with the dignity you have and respecting it.

I have called this chapter Shame and Perfectionism because, while all of the issues I write about in this book go together, these two do especially. Perfectionism is an exhausting defense against shame. If you are perfect all the time, or convince yourself that you must be, you feel you are not vulnerable to shame. It is not our task in life to be perfect, but to learn and to use our life lessons to become better and wiser. We cannot be perfect. If we were, what point would there be to our lives? It is the shame people fear by not being perfect that is the real issue.

Many people have been humiliated and shamed when they didn't meet parental expectations. It is one of the most difficult things in life to realize that parents are just people. When we are small, they have so much power. When my daughter was in the first grade, she once hit another child. This was not anything unusual for the childhood experience as there was always someone hitting someone else. She came home and told me about it, covered her face with her hands, and started to sob as she told me about her time out. She had hit another girl on the arm. I said to her, "We have all done things like that and you are not a bad girl. You're like all other kids and now you have done something like everyone else." I then asked her about the hit, if she had tried to poke the other girl's eye with a pencil or hit her with something heavy that could really hurt. At first she was appalled and said *"No!"* Then she laughed, and I said, "You would never do that stuff, would you?" to which she replied, "I would *never* do that!" She went on to tell me that she hit the child on the arm, a girl who had been hitting her a lot. She said that her teacher was angry at her, and I told her that, of course, they can't have a free-for-all, with kids hitting each other, but, nevertheless, she wasn't a bad girl and she hadn't done anything all of us hadn't done. I told her she would make other errors in judgment on her way to growing up.

She never did this again, but she thanked me for years after this incident for telling her she was not bad. It was clear that my letting her know that she was still a good person had a large impact on her, and helped her to know that one thing didn't make her a bad person. This message brought her back into the human fold.

Even an incident like this can make a child feel terrible about herself. My daughter came with a lot of shame. We adopted her at the age of five and a half from South America, but my husband and I were determined to do what we could to help heal the sense of shame in her and not to feed into it. Yet I have known many people who grew up with their biological parents with no disruption who were made to feel absolutely terrible about a normal childhood transgression, and they continue to pay the price for all that shame.

Whatever has happened to you, you can feel indignant for the small child you once were. You do not have to be perfect to avoid facing the shame that resides in you. You are reading this book; I believe you have the strength to face this. When you do, the perfectionism will considerably lessen or go away.

"Lennie" told me that he thinks of whatever he does as an extension of himself, and that if it is not perfect he feels he is terrible. Underneath the "terrible" fear is the Abyss discussed in the last chapter, but for now it is important to note that Lennie could not distinguish himself from anything connected with him. If company was coming, he had to do a major cleaning job in his home. It had never occurred to him that if anyone judged him for having a messy house, he might not want those people in his life. He could not think in terms of degrees of importance.

There were public and private ways to try to be perfect. While the conscious part of Lennie's mind was concerned about criticism from others, he came to see that he didn't need others to evoke that same feeling. That inner critical voice can be of the mother, father, teacher, anyone, but it is now yours. It took some time for Lennie to see that he was not his job, his home, his tasks, but that those were things he had or did. In one session he asked me "But aren't the things we do a reflection of us?" I replied that reflections are just reflections, and that some are pretty insignificant. I told him that his favorite kind of sandwich is a reflection of him as well, but that I wouldn't do too much with that.

As we have seen, a fear of criticism is very closely related to shame and perfectionism. While consciously people dread criticism from others, they forget that they don't need others to evoke the same painful feeling. They have internalized the person shaming them and can do it all by themselves. Think about why criticism, if true and well-meant, has to be so terrible. If you are driving and go the wrong way and the passenger points this out, is this so bad? Isn't it the self-criticism you engage in that is so problematic for you? Just realizing this is a huge step. People who have been on the path of greater self-awareness will say to me, "If I don't do what I planned to do, I know I'll beat up on myself." While people who make these comments still have much work to do, they have done a lot so far, because they recognize that the "shamer" resides within themselves.

If someone criticizes you and you don't agree, it doesn't hurt. When I was in graduate school, there was a young woman who asked people for help with a lot of different things. She wanted me to help her with her resume right before major exams and was angry that I said I could only do it afterward. Later, she had a baby, and she said to a friend of mine angrily, "I have so much to do and no one helps me with anything!" My friend, who has issues of shame but knew this sense of entitlement and anger were absurd replied, "Well, you chose to have a baby now and we all have things to do. Some of us have children, parents, jobs, money problems, a lot of studying to do...Why do you feel everyone owes it to you to do your work for you when we are all in a stressed time of life?"

This friend laughed as she told me about this. She added, "I know I beat up on myself a lot, but this was so stupid, I felt like laughing." This woman had asked my friend for huge, impossible favors that basically involved leaving her own life and helping with hers, things that were out of the question. Thus, when the criticizer doesn't provoke an issue you already have, it doesn't hurt. When it resonates, it does.

In my former office, I used to keep candy in a dish for my clients. Sometimes when I was in the inner office and no one was with me, I would open the door to the waiting room to greet the newcomer and see a client with a hand in midair on its way to the candy dish. Invariably, people would at first apologize and get embarrassed. I would tell them that it was there for *them* and that there was nothing to apologize for. This led to discussions with many people about feeling like a child in the cookie jar.

How often do parents use shame when a child wants to take something that they would enjoy? This is not always malicious, but some parents are themselves embarrassed when someone enjoys something due to their own shame, and they inadvertently pass this on. My clients who did this were able to see how they shamed themselves and felt like they were doing something they somehow shouldn't, which must have been a very old feeling because they intellectually knew that the candy was for them.

I am not talking about cases where someone speaks to you in a horrible way or embarrasses you in front of someone else. But, if someone close to you points out an error or asks a constructive question that may point out an error, why should this have to hurt you? Maybe the criticism is just a question or is made with good intent. Even if someone does try to make you feel defensive, if you refuse it cannot go very far. If you agree and say something like, "Yes, it was a very stupid thing to do and I'm sorry," there is not much the other person can say. If something else is said, you can say something stronger, but when he or she sees how you own it, there is nothing left for them to say.

What is wrong with making a mistake, with doing something stupid, with not understanding something? We have all been there. Being able to say this to yourself will be very helpful. Like my daughter, you are simply part of the human fold. I have probably made millions of mistakes and will make more, and that is just part of life.

This leads to a discussion of things that really matter versus areas that I call morally neutral. I had a client named "Ali" who lived by herself and would feel incredibly guilty and ashamed if she didn't clean her apartment and instead used her time off doing something more enjoyable. I asked why she felt so badly about herself, and she said she couldn't have people over with the shape her apartment was in. I explained that that was a natural consequence of her decision not to clean her apartment, but why did that make her *bad*? Ali was intelligent and well-educated, by the way, but as my own analyst used to say many years ago, "The intellect plays an unimportant role in how we feel and what we do in most things." I asked her about how she treated her pets, and she responded that I knew very well she was responsible, loved them, and was very good to them, as they were to her. I asked her if not cleaning her apartment was in the same category as being unkind to an animal, a sentient creature. She looked shocked, and said of course they weren't the same, but that she hadn't thought like that before.

This woman recognized that she herself was the shamer, but she considered all decisions to possibly involve major transgressions, when not cleaning her apartment harmed no one, but just meant she would have to live in it until she had time to do the chores. It's in the same category as not doing your paperwork now and having to do it later. This is one I'm well familiar with, as I hate paperwork, but after once getting behind for a few weeks and having to spend hours catching up, an even more dreaded task, I learned my lesson and I do it on time now. In this case I procrastinated for three weeks, I thought about it constantly and then it really *was* awful. Still, this does not make me a bad person, and I know full well I am not perfect. If I had made a promise to someone else and then didn't keep it, I would now have affected another person, and that would be a different case.

Many of my clients who have been grossly humiliated and mistreated in childhood have told me they don't like to think of themselves as having been victimized, because they don't want to feel vulnerable. Perhaps no one likes being vulnerable, but the truth is we all are. It is essential in the healing process to acknowledge having been treated badly when that is in fact what happened. The refusal to let yourself remember deep shame and vulnerability is understandable, but the price you pay for not acknowledging the truth is too high. Who wants to go through life being ultra-sensitive to shame and feeling extreme shame over situations that are not necessarily that important? Do you want to limit your thoughts and desires and aspirations in order to avoid shame and related feelings?

Remember, everyone has suffered humiliation at one time or another. It is very important to acknowledge the truth of your past, instead of dreading the same emotion in your present and future in all kinds of situations. Remember, these situations can be recalled without losing your dignity. Realize that people who are cruel attack their own dignity, as if they are telling the universe to take it back, that they don't want it.

Is hurting someone or breaking your word when someone badly needed you to keep it the same as not doing the dusting in your home? Is taking a shortcut when you make dinner the same thing as belittling someone and causing an emotional scar? Is using a confidence someone shared with you as a weapon when you are annoyed with that person the same as not making your bed in the morning? As you can see, it is crucial for your peace of mind to stop driving yourself crazy, and to begin to see the difference between morally-neutral issues and issues that certainly do carry a moral weight.

How can you be perfect? Is it not better to try to be the good, decent person that you are, and to prioritize? I know this is difficult and I know that the sense of shame, of being bad, lurks right under the surface – but this is a start. Don't you want to distinguish between a person's character and little things that don't really matter?

Exercises

Exercise 1

Pretend that you have a lot of money and are famous, and everyone goes out of their way to treat you well and ask your opinion because of this. Imagine that they don't really understand you or care, but are going by the superficial circumstances. Now imagine that you are the same person who has lost everything, and you are ignored, "invisible" to your old friends. Focus on your feelings and recognize that you are the same person. Now do the same with your formal education, where you are from, what you look like. Keep recognizing what is the same about you. Try to get in touch with your essence.

Keep in mind that our society does not go by essence but by superficial things, and that what I am asking you to do is to go beyond that. Picture other people whose characters (or essences) you like and don't like, and place them in different situations and see that their essences are the same. You will need to do this exercise for a long time, even years, but the gratifying results it brings are truly worthwhile.

Exercise 2

Think of a sick or wounded person you have known. In your mind, see the person, feel compassion, and know that whatever state the body is in, the person's essence is intact. Think now of yourself, your body, and of the divine spark in your essence. Keep seeing yourself in your mind with your dignity, with compassion, love, and respect.

Exercise 3

Think of and write down an example of when you were shamed for something you did or didn't do as a child. Now imagine the same scene as if you were watching a child who is not you. Feel compassion for the child, perhaps indignation, and give comfort. Now go back to yourself and imagine the scene again and give compassion and comfort to the child you once were. Now focus on how you have internalized the one shaming you and now do it by yourself, and how you want to stop. Give yourself the same compassion you would give to someone else.

Exercise 4

Think of and write down a mistake you have made as an adult or something you failed to do. Was it morally neutral, like cleaning an apartment, or was it something like hurting someone's feelings? Give yourself permission to sometimes not be perfect, especially in the morally neutral areas. Think of the consequence of your behavior.

Exercise 5

Think of an argument you had with someone close to you in which you were at least partially wrong. Imagine apologizing with a full heart and humility, acknowledging to the other person that you know you were wrong and are very sorry. How does this feel?

Exercise 6

Imagine some mistakes you either have made or could make when you are in someone else's presence. Note the criticizer within. Now think of others who have an easier time than you do admitting that they have done something "stupid," people you still like and respect. Now go back and imagine your own mistake and try to get comfortable with some of the mistakes you really have made in the past. Imagine someone criticizing you, and that you are "owning" the error, before they can criticize it. Feel the empowerment of owning up to mistakes.

Exercise 7

Make up a few statements that you say to yourself every day. Here are some examples:

- It is all right to sometimes feel sad when I remember being shamed, but I prefer to make room for that sadness than to feel shame all the time for many different things.

- I still see and respect the dignity of others who have been shamed or hurt or are ill. I have compassion and empathy for them and for myself and the times I have felt shamed.

Chapter 3

Rigidity & Black-and-White Thinking

Rigidity and black-and-white thinking relate to perfectionism, and these are all spokes in the PCS wheel of traits. Although these traits are experienced as different, they are all reflections of the same hurt – the dynamics at the hub of the wheel – and there will be overlap among them. For PCS people, thinking in shades of gray can be extremely difficult. In the last chapter we looked at morally-neutral actions versus ones that can cause pain to another. In this one 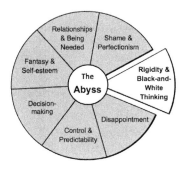 we will look at matters of degree and at the "gray areas" that many decisions fall into.

At the outset let me say that there are issues where black-and-white thinking is perfectly appropriate. Killing, robbing a bank, breaking into a home, or violating the rights of others are not morally neutral. They are wrong. When I refer to "degree" I do not mean to suggest that psychopathic actions are acceptable in any way. I *am* suggesting that life often presents us with gray areas, which are very important to consider in making mature choices. People are not saints, and most people considered good by common standards also have negative traits. So in looking at rigidity and black-and-white thinking, we must always keep in mind that there are universal standards about what is simply unacceptable. Yet we all need to not personal boundaries for what *is* forgivable, and here we will not agree, as different things bother different people.

Some find lateness completely unacceptable, for example. I always try to be on time, and usually arrive a little early for appointments. I know not everyone is like this, but I am most comfortable being this way. Once a woman I had known for several years told me that she strongly felt that lateness was always *wrong* and showed a lack of respect for other people. One day we had planned to meet for lunch and I just couldn't seem to get out of my office. Things kept happening. My phone rang and I answered, fearing an emergency, then I got stuck in traffic. I called ahead and told my friend that I would be twenty minutes late. She was extremely angry with me and, even though I explained and apologized, she remained angry and couldn't forgive me.

I came to see that being late made me a bad person in her eyes. The association in her mind between "people who arrive late" and lack of respect and consideration for others was firmly set. If she forgave me, then what would keep her from ever being late herself? Right is right and wrong is wrong, and I clearly fell into the "wrong" category. We struggled through a lunch where she kept giving me the cold shoulder, while I thought sadly about how we probably wouldn't be seeing each other again, which was in fact the case. I didn't mind apologizing, but I minded the rage and lack of forgiveness. I recognized that I had broken a *rule* and that circumstances didn't count.

Now, it makes sense to distance yourself from someone who really does something to hurt you, but that was not the case here. If you have strict rules for everything, even things that are basically neutral or not really so terrible, you will be a lonely person. I finally left the lunch very much annoyed myself, and that was the end of our association. Though I have missed this woman from time to time, and she no doubt has missed me, it was just a matter of time before circumstances occurred that caused one of her rules to be broken.

I must interject here that traditional religious beliefs can also cultivate this way of thinking. Many in our society, and some of my clients, have grown up being taught in Sunday school that even a minor transgression opens the door to a major one – worst of all to one of the "Seven Deadly Sins." To give Christianity's founders a break, maybe they just wanted people to be more thoughtful about their behavior. This is a good thing. But down through the centuries this way of thinking has been carried to an extreme. Some denominations warn that just *feeling* a particular feeling is as bad as committing the sinful act that it might lead to – thus, Jimmy Carter's famous admission that he had repeatedly committed adultery because he had looked at many women with lust in his heart. While the rigid, black-and-white thinking I'm talking about here might be encouraged or reinforced by this kind of teaching, its source lies elsewhere.

Very often this rigidity comes from a fear about oneself. My former friend was not a bad person and neither am I. But she clearly had a fear about living up to her own standards and promises, and felt she had to be as stern with herself as she was with others – and this meant no exceptions. No doubt, she had had some difficulty with lateness in the past, or more likely, there was something she associated with lateness, and this ran deep for her. Still, when people fear something in themselves they often ward off this fear by extreme condemnation of others, and they then feel in the safe zone of the way they want to think of themselves. But this shows a lack of awareness and cannot lead anywhere good. I can guarantee that this friend judged and condemned herself much more harshly than she did me, and that this is what drove the behavior.

The matter of degree is not an easy one to figure out. What about people who are late *all* the time? I have friends like that, and while it is annoying, the friendships are valuable to me and I overlook this; there are others who just couldn't. What about people who brag to feel important? Can you overlook it if the rest of the relationship is positive? Again, I am not talking about manipulation or psychological games – severe dysfunction that is unacceptable or should be – but the more normal things people do. If one person is very neat and the other is messy, certainly those two should not share an apartment, but would you want to reject someone if it didn't affect you in any major way?

I recall a client who had gotten involved with a strict religious group that ended up being extremely closed and controlling, and she suffered a great deal. She told me that when she first realized that she disagreed with them and wanted to get out, she couldn't face what was ahead and instead became even more fanatical, criticizing other members for not being zealous enough. She did eventually get out, but the stage she went through is a perfect example of how rigidity and extremism are about oneself. She clung harder and harder to something in order to avoid a feared change.

You need to accept that we all are attracted to different traits, sometimes ones similar to ours and sometimes ones that complement us. If you are too tolerant you can end up being mistreated, and if you jump on each non-malicious fault people have, you will have no friends. You need to draw your own line between acceptability and unacceptability. I once had an acquaintance who was a good, kind person, but she always yelled, got very excited, and tended to lecture. She was very bright, and perhaps her job as a lecturer influenced how she related to people. After all, she was used to lecturing to others in a loud voice.

After several get-togethers, I recognized the incompatibility, as I dislike that level of intensity and high volume, which felt abrasive to me. She was a good person, and I still think of her in a positive way, yet, I didn't enjoy her company. Similarly, I knew someone who loved to kid around and who was very funny, and in our brief lunch engagements I preferred to discuss real topics rather than be entertained. A mixture would, for me, have been ideal. Again, there were no hard feelings, but I think we both recognized the incompatibility.

Often, people with PCS traits have difficulty acknowledging when someone is incompatible with them. They feel guilty if there is someone they are not comfortable being with and may even feel they need to find a more significant fault in order to back away. After all, aren't you supposed to like nice people? All of them? Well, not necessarily, and it is really all right to not be compatible with someone. You do not need to hate or dislike someone to back away. In fact, it is important to distinguish between traits you can't stand and things that are really wrong. Likewise, when something that rubs you the wrong way is really wrong, there are degrees of wrongness.

We all have flaws and will continue to. If you condemn yourself, it makes it hard, if not impossible, to forgive others. It is up to you to decide which people you want in your lives – but remember, they are not you. Maybe you are not spontaneous; that might get on certain people's nerves if they mainly operate that way. You could have a relationship with that person if you are open, saying that you have trouble when things are not planned, that that is just how you are, and will be happy to make plans some time. In any case, you need to think about rightness and wrongness and degree, and then about personal compatibility.

We are all drawn to different types of people, which is normal and as it should be. It is all right to not be compatible with someone, and there should be no guilt or shame over this. We all have things we don't want to tolerate. Yet, when looking at matters of right and wrong, black-and-white thinking can be very limiting, as can rigidity. For example, one client told me that she had invited someone to go somewhere and had called several times, but the other person said she was going to work at home and was busy. The client then ran into someone who had seen the friend out and about, and realized that she had lied. My client said, "I hate lies and this was *wrong*!"

I explained to my client that perhaps she had been giving too many invitations, and her friend, not wanting to hurt her feelings, found it easier to tell a small untruth to keep the friendship and not anger or hurt her. My client at first repeated that she hated lies and liars, and one lie made this friend a liar. She was tempted to end a friendship she very much enjoyed. This is black-and-white thinking, and one little lie to ease someone's feelings does not make a liar – one who lies most of the time. This is rigid, black-and-white thinking. You may think this way and no doubt have, and this relates strongly to your fear of being something or someone other than what you really are – your fear of the Abyss. This kind of thinking totally eliminates forgiveness and gray areas, which is most of life.

"Nina" was a young woman who had a rigid, black-and-white system of rules that told her she always had to be fair. She came to me asking for help in breaking up a relationship that was only a couple of months old, one with a young man who sounded quite disturbed. They barely knew each other, but he was manipulative, controlling, and very dishonest. She took everything he said at face value in the name of fairness, even though it was dishonest and manipulative. Once he wanted to go out, and she told him she was going to visit with a friend. She ended up not visiting the friend and just wanted the time to herself. The young man had been watching her apartment and saw that she remained at home. After this incident, he began calling her repeatedly and going into rages, calling her a liar. His behavior was scary, and raised many red flags, but the way he always blamed her for things made her, in her rigid system, always hear him out and try to prove to him that she was being fair. This, of course, was what this disturbed young man had been counting on. There were many other incidents like this, and I knew that Nina had to end this relationship immediately for her own safety.

The last straw that brought her to me was when the young man wanted her to meet his parents. She didn't want to and pointed out to him that they had just met, were not in a formal relationship, and that it was much too soon for this. He kept insisting, and since he had convinced her that she somehow "owed" him (because she thought she could never be "unfair" under any circumstance), she did meet the parents. A week after that, she tried to break the relationship off, and he went into a rage that frightened her. He said that she had just met his parents and had led him on, using what he had talked her into doing against her. This man was extremely disturbed and was dangerous. Nina, I want to stress, was not someone who had ever been abused in a relationship and was an extremely high-functioning individual.

This troubled and dangerous young man played into Nina's rigid association with fairness, now carried to an absurd level and threatening her safety. She came to me for help and told me that this was isolated, that she was not crazy, and that this did not reflect a pattern in her life. I understood that and gave her the quick version of PCS dynamics, explaining how she *did* have issues even though she was certainly not crazy, but that she met someone who made that black-and-white thinking extremely dangerous. This is very important, as a competent and usually rational person who certainly is not "crazy" can find herself in a dangerous situation if these issues are not addressed; in fact, there are disturbed individuals who "read" people very well and will make them feel afraid or guilty about what their Abyss happens to be.

I explained to Nina that I understood that fairness meant a lot of things to her, but that when one is in danger or unhappy with someone, one leaves. There is nothing fair or unfair about it. She met the young man in a public place so as not to be alone with him, and ended what was really, in her mind, not even a relationship. The young man started to scream and yell at her in this public place, which was extremely embarrassing to her, and she started to leave, as we had planned. He pushed in front of her out the door of the restaurant, and that was the end of it.

While Nina had never been in such a situation, she saw how the PCS dynamics hurt her and caused constant self-dislike, and how she kept trying to be perfect in ways that just wouldn't work. Everything she did was to follow her mental list of what a good person was supposed to be, ultimately to win the approval of a hard-to-please father. The father loved her, but was a PCS personality himself, and wanted everyone around him to be perfect. Nina chose to remain in therapy and came to see which dynamics had led to trouble. In the end, that extraordinary incident helped her to change how she saw herself and her life.

Nina made other strides as well. She no longer approaches others simply trying to please and to prove to herself she is good. She does things for others because she *is* kind and genuinely enjoys it, but does not need to prove anything. She knows that she is a good person and she interacts in a genuine and healthy way, with her own feelings and needs getting the respect they deserve. She came to see that the standard she set for herself was one that was not even reasonable to live up to, and she has reclaimed her life. Truthfully, though her father was not a man given to praise, he never intended for his daughter to suffer as she did. Nina's Abyss was being a person who is selfish and unfair. Her dread of this made her extremely vulnerable, but now her personality is integrated and she does not have this vulnerability that can be manipulated by others.

Some people think that they should always do their best and good things will naturally come to them. Certainly it is true that you should do your best so that you have a better chance of *some* good things happening to you, and there are other reasons to do your best. However, as we all know, sometimes bad things happen. People can shout, "It's not fair!" all they want, but life is often unfair. There are people plunged into deep depression not just because something negative happened to them, but because they played by the rules and life did not. While you must maintain your personal ethics, and we all have moral responsibilities, your ethics must allow for the gray areas of life. Things are not so simple, and to live fully you sometimes have to struggle through the gray areas like everyone else. I know that if you think in black-and-white, you will not only be too hard on yourself, but on others, and you will miss a lot.

Life can be extremely difficult, and I would be the last person to say it is fair. Yet, dealing with tragedy is bad enough without having to rage against a universe in which the unfair happens; this only compounds the grief and makes it even more difficult to bear.

Working part-time as a therapist in a nursing home in the past, I met "Harriet," a woman then in her late 70s who had lived with her sister before entering the nursing home. Her story was terrible. She and her sister had all but paid for their house, but still owed four hundred and fifty dollars on it. Her sister, almost 80, had worked as a receptionist, but got sick and couldn't work anymore. Harriet hadn't worked for years due to health issues, though she was able to keep house for the two of them. Because they couldn't pay, the bank foreclosed on their house. It was a heartbreaking story and one our society should be deeply ashamed of.

Harriet told me tearfully how all of their belongings were put outside, and she was especially upset about losing her diary. She kept all of her things in several bags and went through them every day, which was why I was asked to see her. She would pack and unpack her things, over and over. At the beginning, I did it with her, looking over things as she talked about the memories associated with each one.

Harriet lost everything she had, including her sister, who was in a different nursing home. All the two had now was Public Aid. This lady was in the throes of an acute obsessive-compulsive episode. There certainly was intense grief, but she could not get to it or adjust to the changes in her life, at a point where there realistically wouldn't be another chance to get on her feet and get her old life back. She raged against a world in which she had worked and been a good person, and kept repeating that she just didn't understand the rules anymore.

We shared her rage, truthfully, and who wouldn't feel enraged? But she couldn't get to the grief and kept packing and unpacking her things until her room was a fire hazard, with numerous bags and stacks and stacks of papers, letters, and magazines. As I shared her rage and told her how very sorry her story made me feel, I kept telling her how we can only control ourselves and that she *was* a good person, but that the "rule" that meant nothing bad would happen never existed.

Harriet told me that she had never married because she took care of her sick parents, always trying to please them and never quite achieving it. We did some insight work and she came to see that while trying to be perfect and please others doesn't necessarily lead to good results, she had lived her life as a good person. Her niece and nephew visited her because of all the love she had always shown them. She came to see that while some of the rules and associations she had were wrong, she had also lived a good life that had love in it, and just needed to adjust her understanding of a few rules.

Harriet reached the point where she was able, with a nurse she liked and me present, to throw out some old magazines, clothing she no longer wore, and to keep the things most meaningful to her. She did grieve for the loss of her home with her sister and for what she felt was the loss of her dignity. I was able to help her see that while she was treated horribly, she still had her dignity. She wrote a letter to the bank telling them her feelings, a letter full of proper outrage and, yes, dignity. It was a wonderful letter. She did grieve the life she had known and coming to a stage that frankly, did look toward death, but one day she confided to me that she had been too tired to keep the house, shop, and cook, and that she and her sister had been getting cranky with each other. Now, they had weekly visits arranged for them, thanks to the niece and nephew, which meant a lot to the two sisters.

We talked about which rules she would keep and Harriet decided that she could still be the good person she always was, with or without her house. She had always liked things to be nice and neat, and she helped the CNAs clean up the common rooms every day, for which they were very grateful. She lived for being a kind person and for the love she had in her life.

What happened to Harriet and her sister was, in my view, a reflection of some extremely wrong things about our society. At the beginning, I kept thinking how I could have raised the four hundred and fifty dollars for them to keep the house, but I met her after the fact. In my role as a psychologist, I needed to help Harriet face reality and salvage some good, instead of tormenting herself with packing and unpacking and saying over and over each day to anyone who would listen, "I don't know what the rules are anymore." The nurses and other residents saw Harriet as psychotic. She was no doubt in an acute OCD episode, but when the rigid thinking loosened up, her thinking cleared immediately and she continued a life with meaning.

How some people regard authority is another common example of black-and-white thinking. We live in civilization, and civilization requires rules, which must be respected. But again, it is not always so clear. If you have a job and see someone leave ten minutes early every night can you let it go, or do you feel you have to tell the boss? What if you are grossly overworked? If the situation can't be remedied, can you take a few shortcuts that hurt no one, or would you see that as wrong? A client who had never taken a sick day in years always went to work when she was sick. She had been working until midnight and was exhausted and stressed. She felt too guilty to call in sick even though she was deathly ill. Black-and-white thinking can override common sense. Rules do need to be respected, but we also need to be responsible to ourselves.

One client had a roommate who was very messy and didn't do chores. Instead of recognizing the incompatibility and the need to separate after making several reasonable tries, she felt she needed to see the roommate as a horrible person in order to leave. Her rigid sense of fairness and her roommate's reluctance to acknowledge the incompatibility put her in an impossible situation. Eventually, she was able to become less rigid, and to admit that the roommate was a nice person, but not one she could live with. She didn't need to hate her and was able to remain friends after finding another living situation. Rigid thinking will lead to loss, but venturing into the gray area allows for many different possibilities.

A client I referred to in Chapter 1 told me sadly how he would probably always lose friends from time to time because he didn't tell people what they wanted to hear. He would be brutally honest instead. When I tried to show him a different way, he poignantly said, "I don't *like* being this way! I do it because I can't help it." When I asked if he was afraid of telling even a small lie, he said he was. This brings us again to the fear of the Abyss, a very negative partial self-image, something a person is afraid of being if they drop the rigidity.

As this insightful young man intuitively knew, rigid thinking is not an intellectual decision but one based on fear. After years of working with people with PCS issues, I know that they feel like they are standing on a precipice, precariously balancing – one little transgression and they will fall into the pit. This is what I call the Abyss.

Black-and-white thinking only allows for two possibilities in any given situation – friend or foe, fairness or unfairness, yes or no. Letting go of rigidity allows for so many more options from which to choose. "Anita" had a younger sister she was close to and felt very protective toward, even though she was an adult. Anita worked hard and badly wanted some time for herself, but felt she had to spend time with her sister several times a week. After work she would often drive to her sister's apartment in a different part of the city, have dinner with her, and return home, tired and without time to do her own personal chores or relax. I asked her why she had to do so much, and she said that a good sister cared about her younger sibling. Anita's sister was very irresponsible and Anita often gave her money, bought her dinner, and got her out of difficulties. Yet, the rule was that, to be a good sister, one had to do all this.

Given her rigid system, Anita had no room for anything else. She finally was able to carve out some time for herself, and her sister dealt with it. However, Anita said that, while she saw that she should not oversimplify and think in black-and-white terms, she was still uncomfortable dealing with her own needs versus her idea of a good older sister. She and her sister had been neglected as children and she often cared for the younger one, so she felt neglectful if she didn't spend a lot of time with her. Yet, it was the inflexibility in her thinking that trapped her, not her protective feelings toward her sister. Anita was terrified of being like her mother, which to her meant being neglectful. She was able to keep moving forward and she saw quickly how the problem and anxiety were within herself, not really from her sister. Anita's Abyss was that she could be a disturbed and highly irresponsible person. Meeting her sister's every need was the way she kept her Abyss out of awareness.

With Anita's story, we are drawing closer to the Abyss. We have seen how people engage in rigid thinking and black-and-white reasoning to avoid the fear of being a liar, of being neglectful, of being angry, of being a victim. Thinking about rigidity can be uncomfortable because of underlying fears, and you, too, may feel that one slip-up, one exception, one gray area and you will fall off the precipice and somehow be a bad

person, whatever that means to you. It is fear of an underlying feeling
or self-image that keeps you doing something that is not good for you
or avoiding something you should do. It is hard to eliminate rigidity
and black-and-white thinking just by reason alone. This is because it is
motivated by fear. There is nothing wrong with your brain; it is your
feelings you are protecting. The associations you formed were designed
to enforce the rules you have believed in and to keep you safe from
"falling into the Abyss."

In this chapter we looked at things people are afraid of in themselves
and the associations people have with being less rule-bound. We looked
at a fear of telling a small lie out of kindness for fear of being a *liar*,
like someone in the past who was an abusive alcoholic. We have the
rules, the fears and the associations that the black-and-white thinking
is designed to keep away. Yet you know that you have moved beyond
the rigid ways of thinking. You have seen that, rather than keeping you
safe, this PCS system is keeping you anxious, in a state of self-dislike,
and is taking away your options.

Exercises

The following exercises are designed to help you get comfortable recognizing rigidity and black-and-white thinking in yourself and others,
to have compassion for yourself, and to be more self-aware without
judgment. They are also designed to take you closer to the hub of the
wheel, to the Abyss – the source of the specific fears.

Remember, you should be keeping a journal, and you should be doing
the exercises mentally from the beginning of this book until you feel
you no longer need a specific exercise and it has become a part of you.
Do not, I repeat, do *not* use these chapters and exercises as an excuse
to criticize yourself. In this framework, admitting you have some issues
takes courage and leads to change, so please recognize the courage and
honesty you have shown thus far.

Exercise 1

Remember and write down a few examples of shameful times in our history and the history of other countries when people just followed rules

without questioning them. Note that following rules, while generally a good thing to do, cannot be done blindly and that we are responsible for our actions. Think of and write down either a real or hypothetical situation in which you would have to say no to an authority figure. How would you feel? Use your imagination and walk yourself through. How would it feel if you were the first or only person to see that something was wrong? Think of people you know and imagine how they would behave.

The purpose of this exercise is not to have all the answers, but to become more comfortable with ambiguity, an important task in your own growth. In other words, ironically, you need to become more comfortable with being uncomfortable.

Exercise 2

Write down and think about something you did or didn't do as a child for which there was no forgiveness, that made you appear "bad." Remember how it felt. If you were your own parent, how should the situation have been handled to raise a less guilt-ridden and rigid child? Recognize that this is how you wish you had been treated. Now imagine yourself as your actual parent, and think of a situation in which your parent may have taken a "short-cut" in responding to your misbehavior that made you feel ashamed, or worse, responded out of anger. Can you find compassion in your heart for *their* behavior?

Exercise 3

Some things are wrong or right by degree. On a scale of one to ten, with one being completely right and ten being very, very wrong, how would you rate the following situations? How do you *wish* you could rate them? Do you see a difference between the two? If so, do you recognize fear as the reason?

- Telling your boss you don't feel well when you badly need a mental health day or a day of rest.

- Studying enough to get at least a B in a subject not crucial to your goals, but not going all out to insure an A.

- Telling someone a confidence someone told you that is very private.

- Telling lies about someone.

- Making fun of someone and encouraging others to do the same.

- Writing a report for work the night before because you know you can get it done and do a good job.

- Hurting someone's feelings or being unfair and not apologizing for it.

- Saying no to a favor someone asks you to do because you just don't have the time for it.

Exercise 4

Think of and write down three examples of something annoying to you and three examples of something you think is wrong.

Exercise 5

Think of and write down at least one type of situation in which you are rigid. What is the fear behind it? Better still, write down a few examples and identify the fear behind each one. Know that you are facing your issues and that it takes a lot of courage to get free of your fears.

Exercise 6

Think of two times you needed to forgive someone and two times you needed to be forgiven, whether or not this was verbalized. What feelings do you have about these situations? Can you forgive yourself? Is your view from having read this book so far different than it was before you started?

Chapter 4

Disappointment

Disappointment is a major issue for those with PCS dynamics. Why? One reason is their tendency to put people on pedestals, and to feel that they themselves need to live up to an idealized standard as well. Disappointment, perhaps because it is such a big myth-shatterer, presents a major obstacle for some – whether it's *being* disappointed or disappointing someone else. And yet disappointment is a very important and necessary part of life.

Needless to say, fantasy always comes off better than reality. Fantasy has an important purpose in life, and I have devoted a later chapter to it for that reason. Our fantasies can help motivate us to achieve our hopes and dreams and can provide much needed relief when things are rough. Some excellent ideas are born of fantasy. The problem comes when you believe that you or others somehow must live up to your fantasies. Disappointment is related to false ideas of an idealized self and idealized others. Both need to be seen as perfect, making disappointment inevitable. While related to perfectionism, the dread of being disappointed or disappointing someone else is important enough to be treated as its own issue.

In any life situation, there are and will be imperfections. We always have fantasies about new situations and are bound to experience some letdown when faced with their reality. This kind of natural, inevitable disappointment is very different from the disappointment that stems from a serious incompatibility between your expectations of others, based on rigid rules, and how people are in actuality. In addition, there's the disappointment that comes from behavior that falls outside our boundaries of acceptability. It is very important to look at these different kinds of disappointments, and to figure out in any given case where our disappointment is coming from.

In the last chapter we talked about personal boundaries between acceptable and unacceptable behavior and about personal compatibility, which relate very much to the issue of disappointment. Given that nothing is perfect, you must always – when taking a job, renting an apartment, having a relationship of any kind, or in any life situation – determine whether the flaws you see fall inside or outside the realm of acceptability, and if there is a basic compatibility. You need to order your priorities and have them straight, so that you don't go into or remain in a situation that is simply toxic for you.

For example, some of my hardworking clients have described jobs at which they begin at eight in the morning and where employees do not start making motions to leave until seven in the evening. These clients didn't mind working overtime for special situations and projects; however, they wanted new jobs where showing willingness to work didn't mean staying late every night. Taking a different job without finding out if this is the case could lead to serious, but normal disappointment, though one that would basically ruin the job.

When interviewing for a new job, they had to ask whether overtime was the norm, even though they were afraid of the impression this would make. One client said that her interviewer told her that she was "working on" having the people under her leave at six in the evening, suggesting that my client would be perceived as lazy if she left at five. To a lesser degree, having a job one loved except for a few tasks that were unpleasant, such as paperwork, would also be disappointing.

However, these normal kinds of disappointment are different from those based on completely unrealistic expectations of normal human experience, which tend to be devastating. The latter is a disappointment based on perfectionism – the feeling that something or someone must be perfect, or that *you* must be. This is the type of disappointment that the PCS personality must come to terms with. While we

owe each other consideration and respect, no one has the right to live
out one's fantasies through other people.

Many years ago a friend of mine became engaged to a physician. She
told me that he had become suicidal, having never wanted to be a doc-
tor, but only having done so for his parents – that he had really wanted
to become a journalist. They broke off their engagement amicably and
he entered into psychotherapy so that he could learn to have and live
his own hopes and dreams. The degree of his depression showed his
parents how unreasonable and selfish it was of them to try to choose
his career for him – to live their fantasies through him.

Clients often report that their career or course of study was chosen to
please their parents. I tell my clients that though they may be pleasing
their parents now, they will be working for many, many years, and if
they continue in a job or career they hate, they will be miserable for
long after their parents pass on. Maybe it makes people feel good to
have children who follow in their footsteps, but it is not the function of
one's child to fulfill these dreams. This young man suffered intensely
for a good part of his life in order not to disappoint his parents.

My father was a businessman and often told me that he would like
me to go into the business world, something I had neither the interest
nor aptitude for. He did not understand why anyone would want to be
a psychologist, and made this very clear. Finally, I said to him, "I know
you would have liked having a child who followed in your footsteps and
with whom you could share your career and interest. I can't live a life
I don't like, but I understand that you are disappointed, and I respect
your feeling. On the other hand, I do not feel guilty and would prefer
you not try to make me feel that way. It won't work, as this is my
path, and it isn't good for you either." That was pretty much it – until
later.

When I was in graduate school, I was accepted into a placement he
had heard about and which I almost took. After research and thought,
I decided, and rightly so as it turned out, that a different one would
be better for me, and would provide me with the kind of learning experiences I wanted for the work I planned to do. When I told him, he
said he had been telling people about the first opportunity and how it
made him feel so good. I don't think he saw how selfish this was, just
as many parents really don't. I teased that he could still tell people

I was taking the other placement if it made him feel good, but that I couldn't make the wrong decision based on what he felt good telling people. When we talked on the phone, I would jokingly tell him he had one and only one chance to voice his disappointment, and that we would then have to move on. The absurdity of this was apparent to him and he stopped.

What a silly thing it would have been for me to take a placement that could have adversely affected my whole career and life so that he could "feel good" telling people I was there! I was able to do this because my mother had given me the unconditional love and acceptance children need. Not getting it from one parent was not as devastating as it would have been if neither had provided it. I knew that letting someone choose my career could lead to nothing good for me.

There are parents who implicitly teach their children that disappointing them is a terrible and immoral thing, and that the child or adult child must avoid it at all costs. *No.* You can have love, empathy, and respect for your parents, but you must choose your own path. If your parents want to be disappointed, they of course can have their feeling, but you cannot sacrifice your whole self for someone else. They may even come to interpret their own disappointment as meaning that someone or something is all bad, which simply isn't true.

My father eventually accepted the limit I had set. Some adults are so insecure with their parents, they fear doing this because they worry that their parents will disown them. It is a very sad state of affairs when you always have to please others and live their fantasy, when they don't want you to have your own life and your own happiness. Still, you do have to follow your own path. Disappointment, in and of itself, is just a natural part of life. Though you may have been taught that it is devastating, it truly is not.

When children misbehave, many parents will say that they are disappointed. This unfortunate word choice, while understandable, encourages people to grow into adults who think that it is very bad and unacceptable for their parents to be disappointed in them for any reason. They equate the disappointment of their parents with doing something morally wrong and completely intolerable. Therefore, not only must you distinguish between normal and devastating disappointment stemming from perfectionism in yourself, but also in your loved ones. Are you holding others to unrealistic expectations based on an idealized view of the way things *ought* to be? Are you allowing yourself to be held to the unrealistic expectations of others?

Parents of young children often say they are disappointed if their child fights, talks back, steals, etc., and the child develops an association that falsely implies that you should *never* disappoint a loved one. This simply is not true. Even major disappointments may be of the more normal kind – for instance if you let someone down after making a promise, if you choose to pursue a criminal path, or if you treat your parents horribly. When I say that these are "normal" kinds of disappointments, I mean that in these instances disappointment is the normal, or expected response. But a parent who is disappointed simply because of not being able to live the adult child's life for her needs to get over it. Whether or not your parents distinguish between normal disappointments and those based on not-so-healthy expectations, *you* need to do so for your own peace of mind. You have the right to pursue the life that is right for you.

I can't tell you how many of my clients have suffered intense depression because of their guilt for choosing a job or partner that a parent didn't like. There is a tremendous difference between doing something malicious to hurt others – a very serious thing – and simply wanting to develop your own taste and interests. If you disappoint loved ones by not being exactly like them – down to the last detail – all you can do is hope they deal with their own disappointment while you go on with your life. If your parents used the word "disappointed" when you did something wrong, you may have an association with the word that connotes wrongdoing. However, it is now up to you to decide for yourself when something is really wrong for a good reason, or whether someone makes you feel that way for wanting to live a life of your own choosing.

In the realm of relationship, some people have a strong desire to be with someone who will make them feel good all the time, understand them without judgment, and who will not challenge areas of weakness. Maybe we *all* wish for someone just like us! However, that will not happen. When a relationship is more good than bad and we value it, and nothing falls outside the boundary of acceptability, we have to accept the disappointments and move on, and respect the limitations of others. It is only after seeing the imperfections in another that we can determine whether we have true regard or are still dealing in fantasy. A new person or new situation always leads to some initial fantasy, but the real person will have some insecurities and quirks.

A colleague told me years ago that he once had a female client who initially claimed that she had been having sex with a space alien all day, every day, countless times – and that it was terrific! The woman was extremely unhappy about being obese and led an isolated life. My colleague made it clear that he accepted her as she was, and moved her a bit further by responding, "I don't have a problem with *that*, but if you ever want to be with a real man, you'll be disappointed." His wise response contained a wonderful and crucial truth: If you compare a person or real life scenario to a fantasy, the real person or scenario will seem greatly inferior. This lonely woman broke with reality, and created fantasies to soften the terrible loneliness she suffered – and who knows the overwhelming pain she may have endured in life.

My colleague accepted her, but also let her know that real life will have its disappointments. When she told him that she hated herself for being obese, he said, "I don't care what you weigh. You're a nice person, but I care about how much you like yourself and your life." He let her know that there were other standards of worthiness, and that he wanted her to make changes because she liked herself, not because she hated herself. The theme of disappointment dictated the direction her therapy took from the very beginning. Certainly, creating fantasies was easier than doing the work of building up a network of friends and support, which she eventually was able to do.

Think of the excitement you felt the very first time you went out with someone new. You have an attractive, mysterious stranger onto whom you may project all of your romantic fantasies, and then you discover that this stranger is just a person with his or her own insecurities and issues, as all of us have. A new job may also bring with it fantasies of perfection, and you may imagine yourself loving every minute of this new experience, when reality is quite different. I am not talking about a situation in which something or someone is a disaster and you have to move on, but the normal disappointment of imperfection, as every aspect of life must have. As I like to tell my clients, real love and enjoyment is possible only when we look at the real person or situation and go through our disappointment, for only then can we evaluate whether we still feel love or enjoyment for the real person or situation.

We simply would not grow if life were like a fantasy. So many couples have come for counseling and told me the way each had hoped it would be. Each describes an idyllic kind of relationship and life, fantasies that don't take into account the needs and fantasies of the other person. It is only when you come down to earth, let go of the fantasies, and see the real person that you can evaluate whether what you have is love or just fantasy.

Fantasy is fine and even necessary in its place – really, it is essential for a full life, as I will discuss in a later chapter. One of its functions is, in fact, to help us deal with normal disappointment. For example, we might fantasize getting recognition from a nice boss when in fact the real one never recognizes anyone. Such a fantasy can provide comfort against a world that is not so kind. All of us are limited in our own way. Real people can be selfish, insecure, anxious, pessimistic, and have all kinds of flaws. There are good-hearted people who would do anything for you if only they were organized enough to follow through on their good intentions.

Fantasy is like a wish, a wish that people in our lives didn't have the flaws they do. It can give us the strength to carry on when our needs are not met. This kind of healthy fantasy is not like the fantasy of the woman with the space-alien lover, although even she used fantasy to deal with a terrible loneliness. While we don't want fantasy to take over so that we neglect to take necessary action in the face of a painful reality, in a situation in which no action can change it right now, fantasy can comfort us and help us plan for the future.

We are all package deals. People with PCS dynamics have issues, but also tend to be loyal, trustworthy, dependable, responsible, and ethical, and their attention to detail, while annoying in some contexts, is certainly important in others, such as when someone is performing surgery. Funny, spontaneous people can be generous, humble, giving, and extremely self-aware, but can also be disorganized, impulsive, and unreliable.

Every personality type – and we all are a type even with our uniqueness – has traits that can be strengths or weaknesses. Our strengths and weaknesses have the same root – really, our strengths are the flip-side of our weaknesses. It is up to us to accept the challenge of bringing ourselves into balance, doing the best we can, and using our tendencies in good ways, while developing traits as best we can that do not come so naturally to us. We all have the right to enjoy others for the ways in which their personality types complement our own, and to lend ourselves to relationships so that our strengths may benefit others. This is why people need each other, and why we need different types of people in the world.

In the movie "Good Will Hunting," the therapist, played by Robin Williams, told his young client that, while his girlfriend could not be perfect, the correct questions to ask are, "Is she perfect for *you*? Is she complimentary to *your* personality?" These are wise words. When the young man was ready to say that his girlfriend was "perfect" and that he had destroyed the relationship, he was encouraged to adjust to this reality, to see both her feelings and his own, to talk to her honestly, and to try giving more of himself to restore the relationship. It was not black-and-white, perfect or destroyed, but maybe "perfect enough" that, with hard work, they could stay together and be mostly happy as a couple.

While no one should stay with someone who is highly dysfunctional, violent, or who plays games, on the other hand you can't expect relationship bliss with no work at all. You might be surprised at how many people expect just that. Our culture teaches us that we will find perfection and live happily ever after, when the truth is quite different. Relationships take work, understanding, and personal growth. If there is good in the other person, he or she will still have some issues that you will need to accommodate, just as all people have their feelings and needs.

Disappointment relates closely to black-and-white thinking and perfectionism, so you can miss wonderful opportunities by making false, rigid associations. We all need acceptance, but we need to give it as well, even if a person doesn't have each and every trait we think we want.

Mary was a single woman who had dealt with life circumstances that left her somewhat isolated. She needed to rebuild a social network, and when she met Linda at a party and they connected, she was understandably excited and hopeful, thinking she had made a new friend. Mary and Linda discovered that they had some of the same likes and dislikes, and perhaps both thought they would agree on everything. The friendship developed for a few weeks. At that time, Mary became annoyed and very disappointed when Linda spoke to her about wanting to color her hair. Mary was less conventional, wanted to be natural, and felt strongly that she would never dye her gray hair or try to look younger. She felt that women who do this have bought into society's values and have sold out. She spoke about Linda with bitter disappointment, saying that she didn't understand how they had connected as well as they had.

When I asked Mary why they simply couldn't be different and respect each other's differences, Mary became quite emotional and said that this "hair thing" meant that Linda was superficial in general and could not be the friend she had hoped for, even though all the evidence pointed to the contrary. The hair issue, which had certain associations of a political and psychological nature to Mary, became what Mary saw as a "deal-breaker" for the friendship. Mary had read a great deal into Linda's personality because of the hair issue.

The reality was that Linda was being nice to Mary; they had many interests in common, including political ones and especially women's issues. Yet, their interpretations were different. Linda liked doing things with her hair, and to Mary this meant that Linda had "bought into all the BS of society." Clearly, Mary's disappointment was related to her black-and-white thinking. Because she arbitrarily decided that dying one's hair represented a whole personality, not just one aspect of it, she was ready to dismiss Linda. It took Mary some time to realize that she wanted Linda to be exactly like her, rather than a person who could usually understand her and who could share her views on many topics, if not all. Truthfully, I suspect that Linda was disappointed, too, to see how Mary had made a moral issue out of hair and did not feel like walking on eggshells or being apologetic. If you make something minor and arbitrary represent something that in reality it may not, you will be intensely disappointed.

Eventually, Mary came to see that she and Linda did not have a "perfect understanding," but could be good friends, sometimes challenge

each other's views, and care about each other, without either having
to be exactly the way the other might have liked in fantasy.

If you see more good than bad in a situation or person, you can face
disappointment and accept ambivalence. While it was painful to Mary,
she was able to see that Linda had no truly unacceptable issues or traits
and seemed to be turning into a good friend. Mary also saw that what
someone does with her hair is in the morally-neutral category, not good
or bad. She had associated hair-dying with being highly conventional,
superficial, and even selfish, which was simply not true. She realized
that with her black-and-white, rigid thinking she had labeled some
very insignificant qualities wrongly, and had emphasized them in her
mind as having great importance, when in fact they represented only
a very minor part of who her friend was. Later she even experimented
with her own hair color, laughingly admitting that it was fun and that,
of course, she hadn't changed and was still the same person. Mary's
disappointment was based on extreme rigidity and, while Linda was
in fact more conventional than Mary, she came to help Mary in many
situations in which she needed to be more socially aware.

Her initial disappointment led Mary to a higher stage and enabled
her to have a friend she actually liked for her own traits – not someone
to reinforce her own rigid and overly-simplistic system. The two liked
to run ideas by each other and to give each other broader perspectives,
and became very good friends. This close friendship was only possible
after the disappointment.

Accepting someone else and being accepted without having to follow
a script or being perfect is a wonderful feeling. If you are rigid about
what preferences a potential friend or acquaintance may or may not
have, you will be disappointed. Luckily for Mary, she came to see that
this kind of disappointment was exaggerated because of rigid and false
associations and judgments on her own part.

In the last chapter, we talked about our individual right to decide when
a perfectly nice person just isn't for us, and how we can chose to limit
the relationship to a mere acquaintanceship or to not have that person
in our lives at all. Now that we have considered the disappointment
Mary felt over the "hair issue," we can put both ideas into context.

When you feel comfortable with yourself, and know and respect your own limitations, strengths, and expectations, you can feel disappointed over something small without allowing that to ruin a potentially wonderful friendship or romance. You can differentiate that feeling from knowing when a person just isn't right for you. If there is a sticking point in the relationship, you may want to examine it and see if you are being overly rigid and defensive. Or, maybe you simply need to acknowledge to yourself, "This person is perfectly nice, but we don't quite mesh. I respect him or her, and I wish them the very best, but I have made my decision to limit contact, and that's my choice." Because this book approaches issues from so many different angles, this sort of gradual learning experience will only continue to build as you progress through the spokes of the wheel, and get closer to healing the hub at the center.

Another client, "Angela," worked full time and went to college full time, and had a dread of disappointing others. An excellent student, she attracted the attention of an instructor who wanted to be her mentor, and who offered her special opportunities. Angela had a full life, worked, and was not very interested in pursuing a career in this instructor's specialty; she just wanted to do her best in class and receive a good grade. Angela's full-time job entailed a great deal of responsibility, and she often felt frazzled taking classes as well as keeping up her relationships with friends and family. Saying no to the instructor was not an option that naturally occurred to Angela, who had PCS dynamics. She instead became very anxious, complaining that she would now have "no life at all" if she took on the extra responsibility, which was certainly true.

I suggested to Angela that she tell the instructor that the school was lucky to have such a dedicated person teaching there, and that she was grateful for the offer, but that she was very busy and was in fact pursuing a different path. Angela looked horrified and replied, "But she'll be disappointed!" It was clear that Angela associated "disappointing" someone with doing something wrong *to* them. It took Angela a while to see that, although this nice instructor would not get to mentor the outstanding student she had chosen, her offer was meant to benefit Angela – not cause Angela to sacrifice what she wanted in life – and that the instructor would find someone else who wanted her help.

When she was growing up, Angela's parents told her that they were "disappointed" in her whenever she didn't do what they wanted or when she committed normal childhood transgressions. In our work together she came to see that parents and children do have disappointments in each other, and that this is normal – that sometimes you have to do what is right for you, and if the other person wants to be disappointed, they have that right. They would not be devastated unless they had some problems of their own.

Eventually, Angela did thank the instructor and politely declined her offer. She was alert to the possibility that the instructor would be angry, but had decided that she would stick to what she had said. She was pleasantly surprised that, unlike her parents, the instructor did not become angry.

We do not exist to prevent disappointment in others, to change who we are so that we can fulfill others' fantasies, and it is not their function to do that for us either. However, we do make compromises for loved ones and they for us. Minor compromises, such as where to eat dinner tonight, or what color to paint the kitchen, are a normal part of relationships. Compromises that infringe on our intrinsic sense of self or violate our sensibilities, ethics, morals, or standards in some way are not "compromises" at all. Learn to distinguish between the two, and to understand what degree of self-sacrifice is acceptable to you; the measure ought not to be the expectations of the other.

Sometimes we become disappointed because of the timing of things. What we are wishing for could be standing right in front of something even better. I have had many clients over the years who interviewed for a job and didn't get it. They were disappointed. Then, some time later, an even better job presented itself that they did get. Clients often say to me, "Please hope that I get that job." I reply that I will hope that they get the one that is best for them. Sometimes we'll look back and I will say, "Aren't you glad you didn't get the other job?" They always say they are. If you have your mind set on only one thing, when there are infinite possibilities that you can't possibly know about, you will create your own disappointment.

Many of those with PCS dynamics had parents who were disappointed in their own lives, their jobs, their children, and – more to the point – themselves. Some parents wield disappointment like a weapon, and this one word means to many people that they have failed, that they are bad children, that they are hurtful. Yet we all have the right to pursue the lives we feel we should have. If you have issues with disappointment related to guilt because of not living out someone else's fantasies, I encourage you to work on this and to carefully distinguish between the different kinds of disappointment.

When parents are disappointed in themselves, young children often blame themselves. "John" blamed himself for his mother's chronic disappointment, as he tried to make a life for himself. Then he would become angry, relating how his mother had gotten quite angry with him and made him feel guilty for getting his own apartment, even though he went to see her several times a week. On the other days, when he stayed home, his mother called and said how she missed him, and how his visits were too short – and he only lived about forty minutes from her! She would always ask if he was coming the next evening and would say in advance how the visit would be too short and that she missed him already. When he had weekend plans his mother would be very upset that she wouldn't see him for a few days. She did not live alone, but with John's stepfather, a nice man who sounded like a good husband.

John took it as a personal failure that he could not cure his mother's disappointment about everything. More seriously, his mother could not internalize good experiences and, even as they occurred, dwelled on how terrible she felt in between the visits. His mother had serious problems, but John's problem was that he was taught that he was somehow supposed to remedy this sad situation with his mother – an impossible task and one she would need to work out on her own. However, his mother, a woman who was not in touch with her own disappointment, nor its root, felt it natural to expect her son to take away the chronic sense of disappointment she no doubt began to have during her terrible childhood. She then blamed John that he could not do that, even though he was a very good son and saw her several times a week.

John and I separated out his mother's dissatisfaction in life, in herself, and in him from how he thought of himself. He became his own person, coming to realize that his mother was in pain all the time because of her own early issues. She neglected to get help, and then expected her son to take away this emotional pain and the emptiness she often felt. Her own dysfunctional upbringing did not prepare her for parenting and having realistic expectations of her own child.

John came to understand his mother's difficulties and to see them as separate from himself. He had to sadly acknowledge that, no matter what he did or didn't do, his mother would probably not be happy, and would likely attribute her despair to him, her only child. He came to see this and to tolerate it, and was able to set limits with his mother; he stopped looking to her to say he was good or adequate. He let go of all that. He would visit his mother because he wanted to, not to prove anything about himself or to ward off guilt, and he allowed himself some normal adult privacy. The mother was deeply wounded emotionally. She did in fact blame her son and others for her emotional distress, often attributing it to people not paying enough attention to her. As a consequence, John had gotten into the habit of being more concerned with paying attention to his mother, and trying to meet her unreasonable expectations, than with looking at his own needs. Their relationship stressed his obligations to her, instead of the other way around, as is more normal for the parent-child dynamic.

While this was a sad state of affairs, John came to accept his own disappointment over not having a mother who was emotionally healthier. He came to respect and separate from her disappointment. He knew he was a good son and a good person, and he stopped using his mother as a mirror for how good he was. This, by the way, is what all children do and is totally normal, but with a mother like John's, he needed to be his own gauge of what kind of person he was. He first stopped blaming himself for his mother's disappointments, then later for others' disappointments, and finally learned to make peace with his own. He saw that someone else's disappointment was not a reflection on him, and that he did the very best he could. While he loved his mother, he came to see her as a needy but well-intentioned woman, and began to enjoy more of the good in his own life, even with disappointment. As an extra bonus, when he set limits on his mother – while she was angry at first – she clearly benefited. He told her that he would tell her things that he felt comfortable with and eliminate what he was not, and even she came to see that things were much better. They could relate now without the anger and guilt.

Clients often report that after the initial bumpiness brought on by their new limit-setting, their parents' behavior naturally improves. Some express the belief that their parents seem relieved to let go of the old, unhealthy patterns. Because most of these unhealthy dynamics are un-intentional, parents can naturally feel the improvement, and prefer the softer feeling of this new mode of relating to their adult child.

Something especially sad to me is when people give up their hopes and dreams for fear of being disappointed. Unfortunately, I see this very often. People are afraid to want anything they might not get, so they induce a kind of emotional numbing. This is a kind of emotional suicide. I don't know how many times I have heard, "I don't want to get my hopes up because I don't want to be disappointed." It is a terrible thing to live without one's hopes, with or without disappointment, but some people find disappointment so devastating that it must be avoided at all costs, even if they stop feeling at all. There is nothing wrong with wanting and hoping, as this is part of the human experience. The extreme avoidance of hope is really a turning away from life. It is not living at all and is quite tragic; far better to be disappointed from time to time than not to have hopes and dreams. As the saying goes, "It is better to have loved and lost than to have never loved at all." This expression illustrates the age-old understanding of PCS dynamics.

Another client, "Cindy," went out with a young man and liked him a lot, though having been out with him just once. She told me that she didn't want to let herself like him in case he ended up not being so good, or she didn't end up liking him very much. She said that if she let herself hope that she had found her long-awaited long-term partner she would be disappointed if it didn't go that way. Cindy went on to relate disappointment to shame, stating that being disappointed made her feel stupid. She said that if she had her hopes up and nothing came of them, she felt humiliated. I asked Cindy how dignity could be lost if one had hope and liked someone, whether or not the feeling was returned. As Cindy became more in touch with her own dignity, she had the strength to "hear" the inner voice that said something like, "Who are you to think someone could like *you*?"

As she was able to relate to her own dignity and self-worth, Cindy no longer looked to the affections of a new young man to provide them for her. Shame stopped being a part of her fear of disappointment, and she began to allow herself to fantasize. Cindy is not the only one – there are innumerable others who feel shamed and humiliated just for wishing.

So very often people who dread disappointment are not dealing just with disappointment, but perfectionism and shame as well. When the shame is taken away and they allow themselves to hope, disappointment becomes just what it is – not a feeling compounded by other, more painful ones – and it is not so bad. It is important to note that in Cindy's case and others, the Abyss is also present. This partial self-image is extremely damaged and cruel, and almost completely stripped of its humanity.

Cindy went out with the young man for about four months and did let herself have hopeful fantasies. She decided that they weren't right for each other, but was happy both had done their best to treat each other well. Both were disappointed, but Cindy felt she had had a positive experience. She was not defensive and loved the change in herself. About a year later, she met a young man whose personality was closer to what she wanted and needed in a partner. They were eventually engaged.

Exercises

Disappointment is part of a developmental stage and is a huge part of life. We cannot see all the opportunities waiting for us, and sometimes we need to be disappointed to be available for something better to be made clear. The following exercises are designed to help you come to terms with disappointment and to go deeper.

Exercise 1

Think of a time when you were afraid to get your hopes up, and write down this memory in your journal. Was there a feeling of shame associated with it? If so, was it really a fear that others would see you as "stupid" for wanting something and thinking you had a chance? Or was it your own feeling of being "stupid" that caused the sense of shame?

Exercise 2

Try to get in touch with the feeling inside of you saying "Who do you think you are, to expect something good might happen in your life?" Can you see that this is a negative part of your self-image, not created by disappointment, but touched by it? Remember now something you wanted and didn't get and how this made you feel. Remember also your self-worth and dignity, and give yourself respect for the desire and hope, even though it might not have been fulfilled. Think of other examples, over time, until you can recall disappointments of this nature without shame.

Exercise 3

Think of something you want, whether it is possible or not. Maybe you'd like to be President, but are in your 40s and have never been involved in politics. It may well be too late to do that, but the fantasy does not make you ridiculous; you are simply not prepared. Can you think of and write down something it may be too late for realistically, acknowledge that you always wanted it, and accept this with compassion? Hold the vision of what you want in your mind and maintain your connection to dignity. Know that whether or not you can have what you want, you are dignified and worthy. Perhaps there are elements in the fantasy that are still possible.

Exercise 4

Think of people you love, and write down two whom you have had to take down from the pedestal of idealization. Describe in your journal the imperfections and disappointments. Can you love them as imperfect people? Can you love yourself without the pedestal?

Exercise 5

Remember a time when you were full of spontaneous and innocent enthusiasm and someone made fun of you, a friend or older sibling perhaps. Go through this and recognize that the person who made fun of you had issues of shame and was embarrassed by your enthusiasm. Go over the event in your mind, with extreme dignity and compassion for the child you once were, and try to hang on to the enthusiasm. Why do you think people make fun of the vibrancy and enthusiasm and innocence of a young child?

Exercise 6

Write down three hopes you have. Picture them all being met and then not being met, and recognize that you are the same person either way.

Exercise 7

Recall a time when you were small and misbehaved, and your parents told you, perhaps with the best of intentions, that they were "disappointed" in you, meaning that what you did was wrong and needed to be corrected. Now think of at least one time you associated disappointing someone with doing something wrong or bad when that was not the case. Think of times you were right, even though your parents were disappointed, or you feared they would be. Think of things that really hurt people or angered them, and then think of simply not being exactly as their fantasy would have liked for you to be. Note the difference. Can you start to tell normal disappointment from doing something wrong or cruel? Remember, if your actions are well-intentioned and not malicious, even if they don't please someone, or they disappoint someone, you are still not doing anything wrong.

Chapter 5

Dynamics of PCS Personality & Development

In this chapter we take a break from looking at more issues to discuss dynamics,
the cause of the PCS personality. As you
have been reading this book and doing
the exercises, I hope you are seeing how
issues you may have thought were separate are all intertwined. Seeing this has
taken you deeper in your thinking and
your self-awareness. I designed the exercises to help you become comfortable
with your issues and with challenging
them, to become aware of the fear that
lies behind them, and to develop self-love and acceptance.

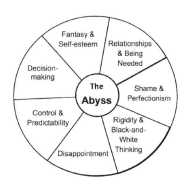

I placed this chapter here, in the middle of the individual issues,
for several reasons. First, the work you have done up to this point
has heightened your readiness to understand some dynamics, and to
go deeper you will need to know them. With this knowledge you can
understand your past even better, as well as what you are experiencing
in the present – how you feel under the surface *now*. Had I placed
this discussion earlier, you wouldn't have had the background or the
growing awareness to put it into context. I also wanted you to have
the benefit of this information to better comprehend the rest of the
chapters and issues. You know by now that they all inter-connect and
form a constellation, and you deserve to know why before reaching the
end.

This chapter has no exercises at the end. If you have been doing the
earlier exercises diligently, you may be ready for a bit of a break, though

this chapter, too, requires your serious effort. You should continue
working with your journal on the exercises from the earlier chapters.

People with PCS issues have all kinds of backgrounds. Some of my
clients have had terrible lives with dysfunctional families and even parents or stepparents who were mentally ill. At the same time, many
have had good, kind, normal parents who perhaps themselves were perfectionistic and inadvertently passed this kind of thinking on to their
children. Some families have gone through crises that were no one's
fault, but which certainly affected the development of the children. We
also can't forget that parents do not raise their children alone, but in a
society where we are all inundated by messages on television and other
media, informing us that we must look perfect, be perfect in school, and
be very thin. It is not clear that society rewards people just for being
nice. If anything, we are given very mixed messages on that subject,
from encouraging us to elicit the envy of others, to congratulating those
wealthy philanthropists who have given their time and money to the
needy.

No matter who raised you or whom you have raised, it is not possible
to do it all perfectly. Besides, what would be perfect for one child would
be disastrous for another, so there will always be issues with your own
parents and with your children. I'm afraid that is as it must be.

Recall the incident in which my young daughter hit another girl on
the arm. My emphasis was on removing the shame and the idea that
she was a bad person. Then, in a humorous way, I showed her what a
truly bad action would have been. My daughter laughed, replying that
she would *never* do those awful things I had suggested. My daughter
knew right from wrong. If this had been a child who had had serious
behavioral problems, was violent, or had no conscience, my response
would have been completely wrong.

So in reading this chapter, as well as the others, I ask you to accept
that, while some PCS people grow up in an environment very uncon-
ducive to healthy mental growth, others do not. If your family was a
good one, or good enough, please know that this is not about judging
them, but about understanding why you developed in the direction you
did rather than in a calmer, more peaceful one.

When I used to teach child development, students would ask, "How do you raise someone with no issues who is still hardworking and honest?" I told them that truthfully I didn't know and didn't think it was possible. No matter what parents do there are negative consequences. If self-esteem is emphasized, the child probably will achieve less. Likewise, some very high-achieving students have strong PCS issues.

You know the kind of home in which you were raised. The highly chaotic, violent, or disturbed ones show most easily how issues develop, and many people come from such homes. You may have been raised very well. The purpose of this chapter is not to condemn anyone's parents. Remember, everyone has issues, and there are many different reasons these issues develop. Also understand that it is not just about how your parents treated you, but your subjective response to them – it is possible to receive a well-meaning message or action as threatening or alarming in some way. As the saying goes, "We know what we give, not what the other person receives."

So do not feel threatened by examples of families that are not like your own, although for many readers, they will be. It is also important to remember that no two siblings share the same set of parents. Your mother might have been indulgent with you, the straight-A student, and very strict and "unfair" with your brother, the class clown. Your father might have shown him preferential treatment, as they shared a love of baseball and crude humor, while he made fun of you for your lack of a sense of fun. This explains why you and your siblings have such different ideas about your parents, and also accounts for some of the differences we see between siblings.

In addition, the parents you have today are not the same parents you had as an infant, toddler, pre-adolescent, teenager, or early adult. Just as we constantly must adapt to our environment, parents must adapt to the changes in their children, as they grow older. When I listen to my clients' accounts of their childhoods, I can often tell when someone's mother or father was a very gentle and warm caregiver when their children were very small, and when they became more challenged once the children were old enough to talk. The reverse can also be true.

As I said earlier, you do not need to meet the criteria for any specific diagnosis to understand the kind of suffering that PCS issues cause. I have worked with many people filled with shame, guilt, and intense anxiety, and these clients often have a sense of exhaustion, self-dislike, and a dread of mistakes. They sometimes have a fear so great that it stifles any creative or original thought. Often, they simply don't know what they want to do in life. After all, when so many thoughts are under repression, who could hear a distant inspirational voice?

Cruelly, too many feel that unless they can select the "perfect" career and excel in it, they will be miserable failures in life and just can't decide at all, as a part of their personality is just waiting to chastise them severely for their shortcomings. It has always been heartbreaking to hear clients say to me, "I'm just so tired." They badly need to rest, but they can't escape from themselves.

The PCS people I have worked with clearly never internalized the idea that they were good enough to be loved just as they are, without intense effort – without being perfect. People who are rigidly perfectionistic don't feel perfect at all underneath. Many of them grow up avoiding either physical or emotional blows, terrified of the pain and humiliation any vulnerability would bring. Others feel so little control over a scary and chaotic life that they try, in childlike ways, to impose some sense and order in a little piece of their world. At least then some things can be controlled and made predictable.

One young professional woman said that when she was a child, she knew that all she had was her morality and goodness, so she wanted to make sure her system was excellent. I doubt she realizes to this day how extraordinary that was. Most people not only deprived of unconditional love but treated with extreme mental cruelty will come to take what they can from others, not try to build a morality that is perfect. Unfortunately, this is beyond the capacity of a child. People who try to do this see things in black and white and have strict, cruel consciences. However, this means of survival, which often gets people through extreme childhoods, no longer serves in adulthood. How exhausting, sad, and even wasteful to go through childhood and then adulthood in defensive mode. I know something better is possible, because I have seen many achieve it.

Certainly, there are people with well-intentioned parents who wanted the best for their children, were themselves perfectionists, and who couldn't tolerate the process of living and learning in their children, but wanted to solve it all for them up front. They failed to understand, in their desire to protect their children and teach them survival skills, that denying their children the chance to struggle through situations and learn through mistakes carried a high price. These perfectionistic and well-meaning parents still caused significant damage, because their children never developed a sense of self-love, competence, or compassion for themselves, nor did they learn to look at the gray areas of life, those between the black and white.

I remind my clients and remind you that examining your childhood is not done to hurt anyone. It is a private exercise, but one that is necessary for you to recover from your anxiety and stop living in fear of yourself. It always saddens me when I see parents planning everything for their children, from all the extra-curricular activities to their classes, and even their friends. I have known other parents whose small children are only allowed to do art projects, go to museums, or do something else where they are learning. They can never just *be*. It seems that as a culture we have come to value extreme achievement more than character or peace of mind, and I don't think we can blame parents for that. Even young children worry about getting into college, and there is just something wrong with that. Many parents teach their children that they must be the best in everything, with no thought that this just doesn't work out for everyone. Personally, I have more respect for a person's character than anything else, and I think good mental health is more valuable than a grade-point average.

Ours is a culture steeped in pride, but I don't see why this has to be. We all have inherent traits. Some people are athletic, some are beautiful, some are good in math, and some have a kind of wisdom. A lucky few have a combination of these characteristics. But not only do people brag about their own natural abilities, which they did nothing to obtain, but those of their children! When you are given a gift, you don't brag about it! It is how you *use* these abilities and how you treat others that count in the larger scheme of things. Teaching children that they have to be the *best*? In *everything*? This is beyond selfish, and I would like to know where it leaves everyone else.

So, in reading about dynamics, while some of you will relate the examples to some real dysfunction or cruelty in your own family, or perhaps to some well-intentioned mistakes, the cultural factor cannot be under-estimated. Remember that while parents and a person's home life are tremendous influences, so is the culture in which we are raised, where, out of pride, we are taught to do things to be better than others. I do not minimize the task of raising children in such a culture.

Irrespective of these cultural factors, I know many people who have truly lived in hell growing up in their parents' homes, and this needs to be looked at more closely because it is far more common than people wish to believe. Some of these clients have had parents or stepparents who were very tyrannical, scary, and almost psychotic. Some have had borderline mothers or fathers, which is extremely difficult for any child. They were not protected and were taught at a young age to be alert to the feelings of the adult, never developing the idea that their own feelings mattered at all. For the sake of survival, these children sacrificed their own feelings, having learned that they really didn't matter.

The Origin of PCS Dynamics

I would like now to look at the origin of the PCS dynamics. I will do this through examples, and then afterwards explain theory looking back at these examples.

"Alison," who was raised in a home with a violent stepfather, was always told by her mother to keep thanking him when they went out to eat, to let the whole conversation be about him because he liked it, and to cater to this man all the time. The mother would have big fights with him, and when he wasn't home, go to her small daughter for comfort. Alison would let herself recall in the course of therapy how she would arrange her things a certain way on her dresser, and turn around several times, and believed that these things needed to be done in a very specific way, or else she would die.

It is so sad to think of a young child having anxiety of this magnitude and not being noticed or given the comfort she so desperately needed. Yet, she somehow went beyond this and survived, even though she had always been too anxious to pursue the career she wanted. Like most people with PCS personalities, she is extremely ethical and cares a great deal about others. Yet Alison herself was never allowed to be authentic, and felt that no one in her life would care for her if she shared her real self – a self that had a range of emotions including sadness, anger, and grief. She couldn't say no to anyone, because she felt it would be selfish. This gives us a glimpse into the Abyss, taking one extreme to counteract the terrible and feared opposite.

Alison was so overwhelmed by her unmeet needs, she felt that to begin to attempt to meet even one of these needs would lead to a totally self-centered person, completely consumed by her own greed. So, to counteract her fear of the Abyss, she instead focused all her energy on the needs of others, just as she had been taught to do. Her mother and stepfather had always told her she was selfish (an extraordinary thing to tell a small child!) whenever she slipped up and accidentally let some desire of hers be known. Never allowed the normal and necessary self-love we all need, she feels she must just exist for others. To get to the root of her difficulties we had to look at how she was raised, and her openness, courage, and intelligence helped her accept what she had been through, and to lessen her anxiety considerably. She was eventually able to think of doing something for herself and to choose a career.

"Nancy" described a very chaotic childhood with a severely borderline mother. Her parents were intelligent people and looked good on the outside, making things still more confusing, but both parents had a poor relationship with society. The mother had controlling and paranoid tendencies, with an extremely volatile nature. At times she wanted to be affectionate and at others she would burst into rage for no apparent reason. She would swing between leaving the children alone and not giving them breathing space, and always told them how she sacrificed so much for them. Her interpretation of the outside world was horrifying, and the children were not allowed to achieve competence outside of her. There were few boundaries or rules, and those that were in place were enforced only sporadically. Nancy could not have friends because, as the mother frequently reminded her, no one would ever love her or be loyal to her except her mother.

Nancy is an extremely intelligent and ethical young woman, empathic and caring, very kind, and with a quick sense of humor, yet she came in wracked by self-doubt, anxiety, guilt, and shame, and having no idea where she wanted to go in life, or when she was right or wrong, or someone else was. When her mother visited from out-of-town, she created major scenes, with slammed doors and screaming, which horrified Nancy's husband. The mother called constantly, and Nancy would feel sick if she ignored the calls, but became *physically* sick when she actually had conversations with her mother. She felt that she would never be free or able to live a normal life, even though everything she had done was toward that end. With her husband, she felt she could never back down or be wrong. Instead of making amends after an argument, she kept trying to show him how "perfect" she was. While to her this meant being worthy of love, he was tired of feeling like he was always taking the blame. Yet, she told me how terrible she felt when she did something she herself didn't like. To Nancy, taking responsibility was associated with humiliation and with having extreme flaws.

In the course of therapy, Nancy said that her mother would never back down, change, or make any concessions to anyone, and had taught her that if you did, you lost your Self and could not be loved. Her mother had lessons for everything and they were all terrible and wrong! Nancy came to see that her husband was more likely to keep loving her if she did apologize when wrong, and that her mother's system and teachings were counterproductive in relationships. Whenever she set upon a new path in life, her mother predicted that she would come "crawling back." The fear of failure was intense.

Nancy is a woman of emotional courage, openness, and honesty, and this has served her very well in therapy. I knew there were things she dreaded thinking about, let alone talking about, and yet she did just that, week after week, in our sessions. It has been a pleasure to get to know Nancy and to work with her. She is so very much better and is able to look at herself and challenge feelings and beliefs. She still has much more emotional potential, but she has done quite well and much of the anxiety has been replaced by sadness regarding real life events. She told me sadly how she had tried her whole life to be as good as other people, only to find out that many of them do not have anywhere near her level of awareness. Even with the loneliness it sometimes brings, Nancy is committed to living a life with awareness and to being honest with herself.

"Donna," almost 30, made an appointment with me and said that she had a panic disorder that started about six months before. She claimed that things had been "perfect" in her life up until that point (always a telltale sign of lots of denial going on) and that she felt nervous and ashamed even coming for help. I asked her if she felt she should never need anyone and should be able to handle anything herself. She looked ashamed and scared and said yes. I knew we were dealing with a PCS type of person in crisis. I cannot fully or adequately describe how frightened and sad Donna was, but I knew that to get beyond the crisis I had to help her make some improvement in the overall PCS personality pattern, or the same system would continue. In an internal crisis such as this, whatever had worked for Donna before in maintaining a balance was no longer working. Her internal strengths were beginning to fight back, and the old status quo would no longer serve to repress the painful feelings that had remained hidden for so long.

Instead of just trying to help Donna resurrect the delicate defenses she had had in place before, or to help her to get back to her "perfect" life that was not really so perfect after all, I wanted her to be able to use this crisis to heed what her inner voice or unconscious was saying: it was time for the truth. How much better it is to help the whole person than just to try to reestablish the same balance they had before, one so fragile that a single stressful event can bring it crashing down. I wanted so much to help Donna. She was truly terrified and thought that she had lost her mind; my assurances to the contrary fell on deaf ears. I knew we had to begin to explore what had caused her to have this "new" panic disorder.

I asked questions about her job. It turned out she hated it, and needed to look for another one. "For some strange reason" she was unable to work on her resume. Clearly, a part of her did not *want* to work on the resume, and this conflict was very anxiety-producing. Something had rocked the boat in her life, something very painful, but it presented Donna with the chance to be freer than before, and healthier, although she was terrified of changing. She hated her job but could not make herself look for another in the same field; this was important information. It was the *type* of job that was connected to her terrible fear and pain.

Something under repression, something sacrificed and denied, was threatening to come to light – the "boat rocker" – and the only way to end her dread and panic was to help it come to light, to be acknowledged, processed, and integrated. People don't bother repressing and denying happy feelings. Bringing Donna's inner conflict to light would no doubt bring on the sadness of something she hadn't wanted to face in the first place, but it would also put an end to the panic.

Repression and denial go hand-in-hand with perfectionism. Nothing is perfect and no *one* is perfect. The lies people tell themselves can collapse when life presents a major challenge. So often people live out the dreams of others rather than their own, and there are times they simply cannot pretend any longer that they are happy when they are really so miserable. Remember that I said that PCS people are often very kind, overly nice in fact, and worry intensely about others and their wishes and feelings. While kindness is a good trait, people often become kind because they learn that only their parents matter, not them. They cannot *disappoint* their parents, as they have given them so much.

I gently suggested to Donna that maybe she didn't like the work she did. She said that she "didn't mind" disliking her work. I was shocked! She didn't mind not liking a huge part of her life? Her goal was not happiness but "not minding"? And this in a young, highly intelligent and also striking young woman with her whole life ahead of her! I asked Donna if she had had a hope or a dream that had fallen through or that she had given up. She burst out crying anew and nodded, explaining that she had wanted to study a field in the humanities, not the scientific one in which she had gotten her degree. She had a calling she had felt pressured to ignore, and even though she excelled in what she did, she disliked it. She had repressed her own sense of the right career path for her, instead pursuing a career chosen by her parents. You cannot sacrifice your calling and expect to be all right.

Donna went on to tell me how wonderful her parents were, how they gave her and her brother everything; her guilt was intense. Not only did she have to be perfect, but her parents had to be perfect, too. I told her that even wonderful, well-intentioned parents did not get to choose the direction in life or the vocation of their children and that they had made a huge mistake; her guilt was a sign that she was not free to make her own choices. The one thing they didn't give her was the freedom to live and to be herself.

The picture emerged of a highly anxious father and a domineering mother with outbursts of temper, who demanded of her child nothing less than total agreement, perfect behavior, straight As – the works. The mother had a difficult beginning in life. She was a woman who had achieved an enormous amount, and was proud of it. Because of this hard-won success, she felt that she knew how to succeed in all aspects of life, and certainly could be trusted to competently raise her child. After all, how hard could that be? With her eye on career success and practicality, she neglected to attune herself to her child's psychological development, or to helping her to develop or attain joy or passion for life. She knew nothing about feelings or emotions. Donna's childhood was beginning to sound not-so-wonderful after all.

The few times Donna was punished as a child, the transgressions, which sounded very minor and normal, were brought up again and again. She still felt guilty for once trying to watch television instead of doing homework, for example. Not only was she punished, but was made to feel that she was horribly mistreating her parents and devaluing all they tried to do for her. The intense gratitude she was made to feel as a young child was used against her. It seemed her parents expected a small child to think and behave like an adult instead of going through stages, choices, and the excitement of learning how to do different things and claim them as her own.

Donna was in fact extremely compliant, as she was afraid of the terrible guilt not being compliant would bring. She had no choices in actual fact, and was forced to be grateful, happy, and compliant all the time. Her real self went underground. Even feelings were guilt-producing. Then Donna spoke of her real career dream in almost a whisper.

I am glad to report that Donna gained almost immediate relief after bringing these dynamics to the forefront. The truth is extremely healing, as unhealthy dynamics are based on lies people tell themselves, or truths they hide from themselves. Donna understood that she couldn't pretend to herself any longer if she wanted to be happy and well. She told her parents she was changing careers, would pay for school herself, hoped they wished her well, but would do it anyway, regardless. They did wish her well, though she could see their disappointment. This didn't bother her really, because, as she said, this was her whole life at stake. She then faced what her childhood was like with a mother who thought she knew just how her child should live, but knew little or nothing about emotional development.

It was finally time to separate the gratitude from the acknowledgement of her deprivations. Donna recognized that in her romantic relationships she always aimed to please, even if she herself felt desperately unhappy. She would be so busy pleasing that she ignored whether or not she even cared for the person.

There is never just one issue with people. As human beings, the issues and problems we have stretch into all aspects of life. While crises are excruciatingly painful, they are also an opportunity to become healthier and stronger in general, as if the crisis exists to let the hidden part of the mind speak at last.

Donna came to realize that she had a right to her feelings, her mistakes, and her life journey. She told her parents that she loved them and valued their relationship, but would not allow anyone to live her life for her. She went back to school and even found that her schoolwork did not have to be perfect if she did her best. She stopped feeling guilty about knowing she would not be in her current job forever, and was able to look back and see that she had felt extremely guilty just for wanting her own life. She had gotten enough love and validation from her father to go through steps very quickly, unlike clients who had had no support. Her mother loved her, too, but had her own problems. I am so glad she sought help, because she found there were, in fact, options other than continuing to be "perfect" for her parents, sacrificing her own life for no good reason.

Donna had a PCS personality. She had in the past coped very well, and had hidden her own unhappiness from herself until she just couldn't stand her job anymore. She couldn't even stand the idea of a different job in the same field, and that was why "for some reason" she was unable to update her resume. Her panic was telling her that if she did not claim her life, she would not find happiness. Had this crisis never occurred, she would have gone on as before, with her insecurities affecting all aspects of her life, by being able to deceive herself, keeping busy, and avoiding reflection.

Yes, Donna did have a panic disorder, but if she had just been seen as a person with that diagnosis and treated accordingly with an emphasis on coping, the important insights that enabled her to claim her own life would never have been discovered, and true happiness might never have been hers. In other words, her panic saved her life, and instead of trying just to get rid of it, we listened to *why* she had it and what it was trying to tell her. Her life became better than it had been before this painful episode.

People often say that a crisis is an opportunity for growth, and this is a perfect example of what that means. This example also shows why it is crucial to look at *who* has the diagnosis, not just the diagnosis itself. Years could have gone by and Donna could have remained a person with panic disorder, with the reason buried and forgotten. In fact, with many clients, we have to dig for the underlying cause of the panic to really help them. That is why I so strongly disagree with people saying what the "best" treatment for panic disorder is. How can there be a "best" if we don't look at the person who has it?

Have you noticed that in my examples I mention how intelligent the person is? That is because the PCS group of people tend to be extremely bright and thoughtful, and they also tend to have been good students, avid readers – people who have developed their natural talents. It would be wonderful to learn how to do that without the self-criticism and anxiety. In Donna's case, it certainly was progress that she no longer felt like she had to get all As when she returned to school, although of course she did very well.

You have also seen me repeatedly compliment these clients for other outstanding traits, such as empathy, compassion, kindness, and generosity of spirit. Please know that though I do not know you personally, and am not speaking directly about you, these traits of *yours* are equally real, and deserve equal respect. I can imagine some readers coming across these compliments about my clients again and again, and thinking to themselves that certainly I wouldn't have such kind things to say about *them* if I knew them personally.

Again, though it is true that I do not know you personally, I extend these same assurances to you: you are a wonderful person already. It is possible to accept yourself for who you are, and start from there.

Being imperfect will never change, but accepting yourself for your imperfections *can* change. In each of these examples, my clients did not believe themselves to be the wonderful people I knew them to be. If this describes you as well, please take heart and extend to yourself the generosity you have extended to others.

"Kevin" was a very brilliant and attractive young man. His use of language was extraordinary, and with an unusual attention to detail, he related the intense anxiety and unhappiness that had plagued him. He was very concerned about making sure I knew about "all" of his issues, although the same pattern could be seen in all of them. He described a full-blown OCD episode in childhood, during which he received no help, support, or attention, yet he managed to go on. This is an incredibly strong person. He described rocky relationships, was in the habit of comparing himself to others, and he was extremely anxious. It became clear to me that he could not distinguish between doing his job well and treating every last detail as equally important, and he felt guilty all the time. When people liked him, he felt they had poor judgment. He was rigid in his beliefs and would back himself into a corner.

Kevin described a childhood in which his parents got divorced. The mother never remarried and leaned on Kevin a great deal. He went back and forth between the two homes, schools, and lifestyles regularly. The father married a very sick woman, who often told Kevin, when he was quite young, that he was ugly, dirty, bad, and disgusting. The stepmother later said that his biological mother had deliberately made him sick to get attention, didn't love him, and was crazy, and this child still had to keep going back and forth between these two homes. Kevin felt guilty for trying to get along with the stepmother, while the biological mother held it against him that he had to be with his father and stepmother, as if he had made the plans. The father never stopped his wife's abuse. Due to academic excellence, Kevin was given the opportunity to study and work overseas, but the stepmother prevented him from accepting by blocking the call. Truthfully, I always felt like crying listening to the intense cruelty this wonderful young man had endured.

Once Kevin arrived at his father's home wearing a sweater his biological mother had bought him. The stepmother made a huge scene about the sweater being ugly, and demanded that he take it off. Over dinner, the conversation was about the "ugly" sweater, and the father even told him that he didn't have to wear it anymore. The message was clear after all this humiliation – that Kevin and the biological mother were ugly. Items Kevin brought with him from his mother's home were confiscated, though they were his only connection to his mother, and offered Kevin comfort and a sense of safety and security.

The way Kevin had been spoken to would be very hard for an adult to endure, and truthfully, I don't know how he survived the gross mistreatment. He suffered from terrible anxiety, shame, and guilt – really, from all of the issues discussed in this book. He did not yet see that the many issues were really just a wounded center. Kevin told me later that when he asked me if I could help him and if it were possible to change, and I had said, "Of course," he then had let himself hope that this would become a turning point for him.

Kevin, I must stress, is a very accomplished, attractive, and competent young professional. He experienced much difficulty acknowledging the abuse that he had suffered, and this difficulty was absolutely not due to an intellectual shortcoming. He was understandably afraid of seeing himself as an abused and vulnerable child, and no doubt also afraid to look at his three parents in a clear light. Yet, the truth and self-awareness are what heal the wounds, and he did this difficult work. He had created a very rigid system to hang onto his values, because the adults in his life were certainly not capable of providing such values for him. Still, it was a child's system, and like that of all children, no matter how gifted, it was rigid, and the values were very black-and-white. Kevin had inklings of what the "Abyss," or feared self-image, was for him. He said, "But I don't *want* to see myself as a victim." I would reply, "You *were* a victim, but you're not now. It's part of how you got your strengths and your hang-ups."

Over time, Kevin came to see that his stepmother had a serious mental illness and projected her own self-hatred onto him. He began to see where the inner critical and cruel voices came from, within the internal strands of his own personality, and to develop a more and more integrated self. Kevin went from criticizing himself for every thought and feeling that did not seem "pure" enough, to a much greater degree of self-acceptance. He is an incredibly forgiving person, and has managed to forgive his stepmother, who is now on medication and has apologized repeatedly. The more extreme anxieties of perfectionism, compulsions, and shame are a thing of the past, and we currently work on what we call the "finer points." He is well aware of his strong points and enjoys them; he can also enjoy the strengths of other people without feeling deficient himself. Kevin is now a much more integrated person with a strong sense of Self, and he continues to give a great deal to the world.

"Jennifer" is extremely ashamed of where she came from, and feels this shame as an integral part of her, in spite of being an outstanding and brilliant young woman. When she was a child, her attentive father began to drink. He then began to use drugs, lost his job, became abusive, and seemed a totally different person. He engaged in these activities with Jennifer's preteen brother, who followed the father down this path. The loss of her father as she had known him and the replacement by an abusive version who plunged the family into poverty was extremely hurtful. While she was not to blame for anything, she had a poor self-image and a deep sense of shame. She was very afraid of being like her brother and father. She felt that it was too easy for people to change for the worse, and she towed the line in a perfectionistic and anxiety-ridden hell. Jennifer survived by creating a very stern and rigid morality that was almost strangling her.

Jennifer is now doing much better, and has very little left to do in her therapeutic work. She is working on the Abyss, the last step for her and others. The other people I have written about are all doing much better, and I hope you take inspiration and strength from their stories as you face your own fears. None of these fine people had a quick or easy path. They understood that the extreme perfectionism making them so anxious and even panicked was a symptom of underlying feelings crying out for attention, and they were willing to face these sad feelings. They came to acknowledge that they protected themselves from the knowledge of having been mistreated because it was somehow easier to blame themselves than to see their loved ones for who they really were. Some have had difficulty acknowledging the vulnerability of the young child, but all have moved on in a very positive way.

In our work together, we do not simply fight the perfectionism, shame, doubt and anxiety, but note that those feelings are attached to some other very painful feelings. Once these feelings are acknowledged, there is sadness, but not anxiety. It is never easy or pleasant to acknowledge painful feelings, as that is why they are repressed in the first place. What helps is to remember that the worst is already over.

Now that we have looked at some courageous people and their struggles in their difficult development to adulthood, let's take a look at the developmental process itself.

No family is perfect, but the healthy family can facilitate certain developmental milestones in the life of a young child. Unfortunately, there are family structures that not only fail to facilitate, but that can prevent these milestones from occurring. There are many different ways to look at how people develop, but I am going to discuss two. One focuses on one's functioning in the world, and the other on internal, emotional states. They both contain truth and wisdom.

Melanie Klein, a famous psychoanalyst, posited a theory of development (1975b) with two main stages. While two stages cannot explain all the different ways people can develop issues when things go wrong, they do cover and explain a great deal. The young infant needs to feel safe and have her needs met, from physical needs to the needs for affection and interaction, for consistency, structure, love, and for emotional attunement. A new infant engages in what we call splitting, which means they experience pleasure or pain, good or bad, but no in-between. Even the best mother in the world will sometimes take a few minutes before responding to her baby's cries, and this causes frustration. At that moment the infant experiences her as bad.

D. W. Winnicott (1953), a British psychoanalyst, added another dimension to Klein's theory. He coined the term "good-enough mother," which means a mother good enough to let the next stage of development occur. This kind of mother (or father, or other caregiver) cannot be perfect, but can allow the infant to experience much more good than bad. In this way, the infant comes to realize that the wonderful person who meets his needs is the same "bad" person who also frustrates him, and is sometimes late. This awareness heralds a new stage of development, one where the infant realizes that loved ones are not perfect, and can sometimes disappoint, and that he himself is not perfect, but is "pretty good." In other words, attending to the infant's physical and emotional needs allows him to see that his caregiver is more good than bad, which leads to him feeling that he himself is more good than bad.

As he grows older and begins to participate in life, this extends to the world and to other people, so that he can see the world at large as being more good than bad. This is all primitive, but we can see in adult issues that few people seem to reach this second stage, or successfully navigate all the way through it. The alternate outcome of all of this is, of course, seeing the mother, himself, and the world as more bad than good. This outcome is very sad indeed, and will certainly lead to depression, anxiety, and other painful feelings. It will also result in splitting and black-and-white thinking, and explains some of the core issues this book describes.

This second stage marks the beginning of guilt and concern: guilt for having angry feelings toward the loved one, and concern that the angry thoughts could have actually hurt the mother. In order to reach this second stage, or to attempt to get through it and have an integrated personality, the young one's needs must be met in this "good enough" way. A consistent, warm, nurturing and responsive approach is all that is needed. Unfortunately, we see in older children and in so many adults that this was not allowed to happen.

Without this empathic consistency, the angry, frustrated parts of the self can become split off, separated from the whole, and thus represent a feared entity – an internal monster, denied at all costs. Here we can see how very deep are the roots of each person's Abyss, and why it is so difficult even for very bright, intelligent people to find easy access to the underlying causes of their behaviors, thoughts, and feelings.

It is important to understand that perfectionism and extreme idealism are defensive in nature, covering feelings so fragile that nothing the least bit negative can interfere. People with secure attachments to their parents are able, in a good-natured way, to say how they dislike a few things about them and vice versa, and these things are often the basis for humor and family banter. Someone might be teased for being a worrier, or not being able to keep a secret, or not understanding things, for instance.

However, people who have the PCS cluster of traits have great difficulty with this. They have a strong need to see people, both themselves and others, as all-good or all-bad. For this reason, parents and significant caretakers are idealized and put on a pedestal. Even minor human flaws get an excuse: "Yes, I had to care for myself at age five, and my younger sibling as well, but my mother had to work." The need to idealize and pretend someone is perfect goes back to this splitting stage.

Remember, the mother, the environment, and life in general must be felt as more good than bad, for the foundation to be laid for good mental health. This is what gives people the courage to acknowledge imperfections and disappointments. When people can't do this, their inability to integrate their view of self and others speaks to a great deal of fear and pain. The great fear is the loss of the internalized, false image that means so much as a myth in people's lives – yet conversely is the source of such overwhelming anxiety.

Many perfectionistic people find disappointment devastating. This black-and-white thinking – one is either all-good or all-bad – originates in infancy. People who are stuck in this phase, who found themselves unable to move completely into the second stage, where integration is possible, struggle with disappointment for this very reason.

In the normal course, acceptance and integration follow naturally from disappointment. Rigid modes of black-and-white thinking prevent this type of emotional growth. As we have acknowledged, PCS personality types are ethical people; their need to protect others enforces this rigid splitting-off of the reality of their surroundings. As they grow older, they become increasingly afraid of the Abyss. Because of this, the defenses they have erected to ward of their knowledge of the Abyss – the spokes of the wheel – become more and more cemented. Working through the spokes of the wheel makes it possible to heal the hub at the center, allowing you to see that the Abyss doesn't need to be feared any longer; it has begun to lose its power over you.

While some of these people are stuck right in the first stage, and some have moved into the second, but are not quite through it, we can see the tendency toward perfectionism here. There is no morally-neutral ground; there is good and there is bad. Not being perfect means being bad. It also means, sadly, that they never felt the environment was more good than bad, and were unable to acknowledge the imperfections in themselves and others. These children grow into adults who feel that disappointment, a normal and necessary part of development and of life, must be avoided at all costs – even at the cost of an authentic self who is at peace.

Here is what I call the Abyss, the false belief that if one is not perfect and toeing the line all the time, we have a very, very bad person indeed. These children never learn to maneuver morally-neutral ground.

One client I mentioned earlier has chastised herself terribly whenever she hasn't cleaned her apartment, where she lives alone. In spite of a wonderful intelligence, the concept of a morally-neutral area was alien to her, and not cleaning an apartment was nearly in the same category as murder. Black-and-white thinking and the fear of the Abyss take all the wonderful shades of gray out of life. People tread water, never realizing that they can actually stand up and rest. The pain is very real.

We see this black-and-white thinking in fanaticism: My religion is all-correct and yours must be all wrong. There is no room for see-ing wisdom in different traditions. There is no room to negotiate life. This kind of thinking affects all sorts of situations, not the least our relationships with others, who bring their issues to the table as well.

Remember my dear friend against whom I committed the grave sin of being late for lunch? Let's consider her extreme reaction to my lateness in the context of our lesson from Melanie Klein.

In my friend's rigid system, there was no room for my lateness. Rigid-ity is a major component of splitting, or the need to keep good and bad qualities clearly separated. I had entered into the "all bad" category by being late one time. She did not have the tools to continue to see me as a good person after that. I understood this, and even sympathized with her, but I had no intention of entering into this system of hers. Really, if she had forgiven me – and forgiveness goes with the second stage, along with accepting disappointment in a loved one – this would have meant *she* wasn't any good as a person either. It would have been much too stressful for her.

In this type of rigid system, the gray areas must be avoided at all costs. That is why we see some highly intelligent people who fear the Abyss, who suddenly get very, very concrete and literal, well below the intelligence level we know them to be capable of. Remember the wise words of my wonderful analyst: The intellect plays a small part in what we feel and what we do. I tell my clients that when they experience this drop in intelligence to take note; it means some emotional structure is interfering with their ability to think.

I do want to stress, however, that many people who are what I consider extreme perfectionists can be very forgiving of others. They need to learn to forgive themselves, as well. When a parent is strict, rigid, and unforgiving, the child has little chance to learn to do this on his own. However, the adult can do this. All it takes is the courage to face the hidden emotions that cause all the distress.

Getting back to Klein's stages (1975a), the latter half of the second stage is concerned with making reparations. This means making things right, forgiving yourself and others. As I have said, my former friend did not get that far, although most of my clients have, even when there is still black-and-white thinking. Many people complete some of stage one and some of stage two, and are caught somewhere in between. Unfortunately, so many times we hear of children apologizing for some childish transgression, and the parent will respond, "Don't be sorry. That doesn't help anything." This tells the child that there is no room for anything other than perfection, and there are no reparations. The adult incorporates this lesson, finding any imperfection in himself a sign of something almost evil.

In therapy I work in partnership with each client to mend the splitting and black-and-white thinking, and to show them that there *is* in fact reparation for the small and inadvertent things we all do. Degree is of course very important in life situations, and many people with rigid, perfectionistic thinking have difficulty with matters of degree, since they feel that any transgression is unforgivable. We all agree that certain things are not acceptable and certain things are desirable. We all, however, have different boundaries of acceptability.

This is sometimes hard for perfectionists. They think the "sin" of being a nervous person is on an equal par with someone who perhaps does something uncaring and harmful with full knowledge. They are afraid that if they don't put up with everything, the only other choice they have is to tolerate nothing. This too represents both splitting and black and white thinking.

While I understand the pain behind wanting to simplify life and have clear and easy rules, an adult simply can't live a normal and healthy life without plunging in and muddling through all these gray areas. To complicate matters, our own personal gray areas change throughout life as we grow and have different experiences, so we need to make adjustments. This does not mean we were wrong before, but that the old ways no longer serve.

Remember, these black-and-white, rigid rules were made by a child who needed peace, tranquility, and some structure and stability – but what works for someone who is seven does not really work for an adult.

I once had a client named "Joe" with rigid perfectionism who wanted to change careers. This involved taking more math than he did in college. He was very upset, and said that he hated to take something he couldn't get an A in. It turned out to be the best thing for him, as he got tutored, got Bs and Cs in math, excelled in his choice of career, and is brilliant at what he does. Joe lifted the burden right off his shoulders, growing in self-love and in humility.

You should know what your gifts are, what they are not, and where you fall in the middle. Fear keeps so many people back. Really, what would be the purpose of the very hard life journeys we all have if we were already perfect and knew everything? I cannot think of one reason why we would be here if we had already achieved that.

People with PCS dynamics split off, deny, and hold back a part of their Selves. We have barely touched on the price they pay for this, or how it impacts nearly every aspect of their lives. People with these issues, while typically very intelligent, are out of touch with their own intuition. They miss out on the normal struggles and gray areas of life, and are unable to calmly explore ideas, free from unrelated anxiety – not to mention their pervasive fear of minor imperfections.

The PCS dynamics are there for a reason – they protect the individual from the Abyss. However, as this book encourages you to see, these dynamics do *not* protect from the *fear* of the Abyss. The terrible anxiety this fear causes is at the root of each one of the spokes of the wheel – each of the PCS dynamics. If one is not perfect, one can spend each moment compensating for this "criminal" tendency toward imperfection. The imaginary monster within demands these safeguards be scrupulously upheld. Meanwhile, there is no room to breathe.

The false beliefs come in all varieties: If I am not a workaholic I might miss work and sleep in all the time because I am lazy. If I tell a little white lie so as not to hurt someone's feelings, then I am a liar who can't take responsibility for my actions. If I go to a party and have a drink, I will become a hopeless alcoholic. If I admit that I don't like someone, even to myself, I am a terrible person who has a lot of anger. If I ever get angry for any reason at all I will be a terrible person. In none of these myths is the individual allowing himself to be a full, total person, let alone an authentic one. There is no room for "Everything in moderation, including moderation" in these examples.

One of the gentlest people I know thinks he is violent, even though he has never even come close, because his mother told him he was violent if he was resentful about anything. This is the fear of the Abyss, fear that must be faced and not just coped with and controlled. The process of recovery and healing is what I believe to be most important, not the ability to learn even more ways of coping with an already impossible amount of pain.

We see examples of the Abyss in all areas of life, if we know where to look. Sometimes hearing the stories of others and considering their experiences and feelings can be easier to do than looking at your own. Through considering the pain of other people, you may begin to feel more comfortable in looking at your own life. It helps you get used to a new way of thinking and looking at yourself. Many authors and artists have an intuitive understanding of this very common fear in human nature, and we can read novels or watch films in which this wisdom is shared with the audience.

In Peter Høeg's novel, *Smilla's Sense of Snow* (1993), Smilla, the main character spends the entire book trying to convince the reader – and perhaps herself – that she is a tough, crass, invulnerable person, totally heartless and concerned only with herself. The Smilla we get to know is quite the opposite, filled with love, compassion, and the desire to help others, though her fear of being hurt causes her to erect these walls around herself, keeping everyone at bay. To Smilla, it is easier to be rejected because *she* has planned the rejection in advance. This gives her an artificial sense of power and control, and allows her to believe that she is stronger and better than other people, and that she doesn't need others.

The truth is, Smilla is hungry for basic human intimacy, and desires nothing more than to be known and understood by another human being. But she is so afraid of them getting to know her, judging her and rejecting her, and so protective of the imaginary monster inside of her, that she keeps people at bay with this false Self.

The psychoanalyst Erik Erikson (1950) posited eight psychosocial stages that people need to pass through from birth to older adulthood. Successful completion of each stage assures good adjustment. They are psycho-*social* stages, and describe very well how people relate to others and the world. For this reason they are very useful. They do not replace the richness of Melanie Klein's stages and descriptions of the inner workings of the mind, but supplement it with another extremely helpful perspective. Both theories have strengths and weaknesses, and I am not selecting one over the other. Using two different frameworks helps to explain and examine the human state in a richer and more complex way.

I will begin by listing these stages and the corresponding age range of each stage. When we look at types of dysfunction in families and you examine your own issues, these stages will help you pinpoint when some of them were highlighted and why. I do not mean to imply that all people come from abusive backgrounds, and we are not in the business of blaming, but it is still important to have a framework for examining when the anxiety arose. One's *experience* of one's environment, one's constitutional makeup, and one's subjective interpretation of events, all create the end result. Nonetheless, the majority of people have dealt with some real unhappiness. Sometimes it is not a parent, but a stepparent, girlfriend or boyfriend with whom you may have struggled the most. Sometimes there is some other external influence. You have to see what is true for you.

Erikson's eight stages are:

1. Basic Trust vs. Mistrust – Birth to one and a half

2. Autonomy vs. Shame and Doubt – 1 to 3

3. Initiative vs. Guilt – 3 to 6

4. Industry vs. Inferiority – 6 to 12

5. Identity vs. Confusion – 12 to 20

6. Intimacy vs. Isolation – Young Adulthood

7. Generativity vs. Stagnation – Middle Age

8. Integrity vs. Despair – Older Adulthood to Death

As we discussed from the perspective of Melanie Klein and splitting, the infant needs a calm and predictable environment. Erikson would agree with this, though in his first stage he stresses the development of basic trust rather than integration. It is easy to see how the mother's care of the infant either succeeds in building trust or does not, depending on whether the infant learns from experience that his needs will be met and that he can trust that they will continue to be met – that the environment is good and safe.

We have all heard of the terrible twos. Between the ages of 1 and 3 years, a child gets into normal power struggles with the mother. This must occur for normal and healthy development, even though it is a difficult time for mothers, and more so for mothers with problems of their own who might not have had good parenting themselves. This is an important stage, because in opposing the mother, the child is proving to herself that she is a person separate and independent from the mother. This should be handled in such a way that the child learns that she is autonomous and can handle some things on her own. We often see good mothers praising their toddlers for an age-appropriate accomplishment. If the family is dysfunctional or the mother cannot bear to have the child not need her for everything, the child will doubt her ability to be her own person, or to achieve autonomy. The child who is not treated properly or who is humiliated will learn to feel shame for reaching out and trying something new.

I remember in graduate school reading about different parenting styles, from normal to abusive. One example from the abusive end of the spectrum was about a mother who got very angry when the child wanted to try something himself. When the child came to her for help, she made fun of him and said, "I thought *you* could do it, but you couldn't, could you?" This mother felt it as a terrible put-down that her child was growing and developing, so she lashed out in a way guaranteed to produce pain and suffering in the child.

As I said earlier, this stage is very important for people with PCS dynamics and perfectionistic extremes. Autonomy and shame are huge and painful feelings for them. These people have a dread of being told what to do. They often have hostile feelings toward authority, a dread of giving in, and can sometimes pretend to comply with a boss, a teacher, or a spouse, while quietly thwarting what is wanted. It is not a desire to be mean that directs this behavior, but the autonomous self that feels so very fragile and easily threatened.

"Ellen" struggled with severe anxiety and a fear of being wrong or imperfect, though her mother was even more extreme. Even with an adult child, the mother would not modify behavior that was inappropriate. She hurt and mortified her adult daughter, saying she is who she is, will not change one thing, and since she brought her into the world can treat her any way she wants. She caused Ellen a great deal of suffering. Not surprisingly, Ellen, like others with these issues, had a dread of needing anyone or being dependent. The fear of reaching out for something new, and the fear of dependency – whether her own or someone else's – left her in a terrible, lonely position.

As infants and young children, we are dependent upon our caregivers, which is normal and right. As we grow older, we go through a stage in which we need to learn to be independent and do things for ourselves. Once we have enjoyed independence for a while, and if we choose to enter into a healthy adult relationship, we then become *inter*-dependent, meaning that we agree to depend, to some degree, on our partner, and to accept our partner's dependence upon us. This is the healthy and normal course of adult relationships.

Some people with PCS dynamics enter into relationships intent on maintaining absolute independence, and denying that they depend upon their partner for anything at all; others become totally dependent upon their partner, losing their sense of individuality and autonomy in the process. A balance is needed in all relationships. This is the meaning of inter-dependence.

When a child is given mixed messages about dependence, the adult will also feel very mixed-up about depending on other people. It is best not to cling to either extreme, not to be totally independent or totally dependent upon the other person, but to find something in-between. There is nothing shameful about needing other people in your life; it only means you are human. We all need our loved ones to help us, and we can help them as well. This is normal and comforting and helps to make life bearable. We will discuss these issues further in the chapter on relationships.

Shame is also a major issue for those with anxious perfectionism. Some parents humiliate children during toilet training, making them feel shameful and dirty for life. If basic needs are not met, the issue of shame arises for many reasons.

"Darlene" told me that once, when she was a young child, her mother served a very good dinner. Darlene was smiling and eating, enjoying the meal. Her mother then ridiculed her "greed" in front of other family members, and Darlene never allowed herself to feel this type of enjoyment again. She was afraid to show she enjoyed *anything*. Of course food then played a major role in this dynamic, and she learned to deprive herself.

"Sammie" had a mother who was schizophrenic, and the home was filthy. She took on most of her own care and that of her younger brother at a very young age, but she was too small to clean up the whole house or to change things in any major way. They would sometimes eat bread with ketchup because there was nothing else to eat. She laughed in a self-deprecating and self-blaming way when she told me how she used to eat. As she grew older, the filth in the home and the mother's behavior embarrassed her, and she could not have friends over at all.

As an adult, Sammie's home is very, very clean and always well-stocked. It is *so* neat and *so* clean that her friends are always amazed. This is how she counteracts her shame. Her emphasis with her children is to never let them be ashamed. While that is a good goal, it is stressed a great deal because of her own shame. When she responds to something "improperly," she feels just terrible – a feeling always just beneath the surface for Sammie, even though she is a wonderful person.

Many clients have shared with me the great shame of making some small mistake. One client has to do an extremely deep cleaning before anyone comes over, because she is afraid of remembering her mother calling her a pig when her room was messy as a small child. Her mother taught her not to give in to anyone, never to listen to anyone, and never to be wrong, but to do a major overhaul if anyone comes over. It took a lot of courage, time, and struggle to sift through all the false things her mother taught her.

In the Initiative vs. Guilt stage, which takes place from ages 3 to 6, a child should have an environment that encourages his thinking and ideas. He learns to trust his own judgment in going toward things that seem good, trying new things, and taking it in stride if he fails at something that is too difficult. He learns to trust his thoughts, that they are important, and is a happy and active child.

When a child's ideas and questions are treated with derision or ignored, this produces a child with an inhibited fantasy life and a vague feeing of guilt related to being happy, carefree or engaging in fantasy. It is not surprising, then, that many people with PCS personalities say they do not fantasize. It is no wonder that they don't know what they want to do in life, because without fantasy, how can we experiment with different things? How can we imagine the way different experiences might feel?

It is so sad to me how very many of my clients say that they have no idea whether they would like something until they do it. I always encourage them to use what they know they like and dislike to determine this, and they are always surprised and delighted that they already know and have this information. It hits them a bit later that they didn't have this skill that was in fact their birthright. Erikson would say they feel guilty about fantasizing, a vital skill for life.

In the Industry vs. Inferiority stage, which occurs from ages 6 to 12, a supportive and healthy family encourages the child to take some pride in and have good self-esteem regarding her accomplishments, in schoolwork, sports, and in interpersonal interactions. A child who masters the other stages will have good peer relationships, while the child who has not will feel like an outsider and either keep to herself or seek out other outsiders.

At this stage, children very consciously feel like either failures or successes, and in the worst cases will show indifference to social activities and learning. It is a tribute to the exceptional people I have worked with that, in spite of extremely dysfunctional families and often cruelty, they realized that they could learn, must learn, and found needed support from teachers and peers. They are often high achievers, and no one would suspect the terrible anxiety, doubt and feelings of being an imposter they live with.

Although Erikson's first four stages are the most relevant to people with painful perfectionism, and who live in fear of the Abyss, I will briefly describe the others as well. Since one stage builds on another, this emphasizes all that is lost if one's issues are not confronted.

In the Identity vs. Confusion stage, which ranges from adolescence to early adulthood, a person forms an adult identity from her experiences, finding pleasure in learning new things, and trying some of them out to see if they are appropriate for her. When the family has failed to support the earlier stages, people with the problems described in this book will back away from new thoughts that challenge their rigid ideas. People with other types of problems will engage in harmful excesses. A person with a fear of the Abyss will feel so fragile in her identity, she will often fear ideas that conflict with her rigidly held beliefs, as the world must be kept in rigid, simple, black-and-white terms.

In the Intimacy vs. Isolation stage, the young adult should be able to have close relationships, loving friends and having romantic love. Many people who suffer from PCS dynamics can do this, but they bring their own perfectionism to their relationships with friends and partners. They try to show the person how perfect they are, needing the validation and needing to earn the love over and over. The problem is, they have trouble letting anyone give to them. In their need for validation and in their anxious pain, they can forget that the other person wants to feel needed and useful as well.

People like this like to be needed, and sometimes seek out dysfunctional people so they can be the strong and needed ones. They find it hard to need, to depend on someone, to stop controlling things, in an effort to make a safe and predictable environment. They are often very hurt when their efforts are not only unappreciated, but resented, as their efforts allow the other person little chance to develop.

The Generativity vs. Stagnation stage belongs to middle adults and relates to the desire and ability to nurture the next generation. This can take the shape of involvement with children, grandchildren, or reaching out to other people or even helping animals. This can also be expressed by being creative or productive in some other way.

Integrity vs. Despair belongs to the older adult facing death. If one feels life has been satisfying, it is not hard to face death, but when one feels she has missed out a great deal, there is instead a dread of dying. It is important in this later stage to feel that life has been worthwhile.

While the first four stages are the most relevant to people with PCS traits or dynamics, the last two do bear thinking about. It can be seen that the later the stage, the more thoughts, ideas, and feelings are important. As we get older, we look at what we have learned and reach out to others to help them. There is less direct *doing* and more thinking and processing, components leading to wisdom.

We have looked at major developmental issues in Klein's and Erikson's frameworks. These theories describe what people need to develop into healthy adults. In the next chapter we will look at types of dysfunction. As you can see, we are not teaching coping or just dealing with symptoms, but inviting you to look under the surface, to look at the unique, complex, and emotionally-rich person that you are.

Chapter 6

Control & Predictability

People with PCS dynamics often say they like to plan everything, so that life can be predictable and under their control. Sometimes people call them "control freaks," as their desire to control tends to rub others the wrong way. This need to control is not malicious, but simply reflects the fear of the unknown. The unknown contains specific fears for different people, as each person has his or her own unique Abyss. Many of my clients 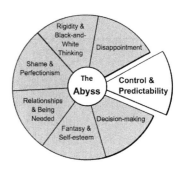 have jokingly yet tearfully said that they wished their whole lives could be predictable, knowing that as they said it and wished it, how very much they would be missing out on if life were this way.

Why do you like to have control and predictability? One obvious reason is that there was a time when you clearly *didn't* feel much control at all. I have clients who lived in absolute chaos as children, who tried very hard to control and order something, which often, of necessity, was the product of their own minds. Sometimes this was a ritual, or sometimes it was possessiveness over a toy or game, or some rigid rule that let them know they could control something. Some people survived their childhoods by convincing themselves that they didn't want anything at all so that they were not constantly frustrated.

"Elaine's" mother has a severe borderline personality. She abused Elaine and her younger brother and sister while the father turned a blind eye. When her mother went into fits of rage, she would throw out the children's toys, and they never knew when one of her rages would strike. They would get new toys for birthdays and Christmas, but were afraid to get attached to anything. As an alternative to destroying her children's toys, Elaine's mother would tear down posters from their rooms when she became angry, so they couldn't get too attached to their rooms either.

Elaine's inability to get attached to others now gives her a sense of control. As unfair as it may be, after all of her losses and helpless victimizations, she had to face the possibility of loss and disappointment once more in order to let herself care about someone. She felt that if she became involved in a relationship and cared about the person, she would be devastated if it ended, but that she would handle it as well as anyone could. The very fact that Elaine has made it this far in life shows what a strong person she has become.

The only problem was that she was afraid to need or to love. When she began dating someone new, she would try to show this new person how "perfect" she was, how upbeat and how desirable she could be. Once she felt that she had succeeded in controlling the way her new love interest saw her, she then entered into the relationship, but would soon show her partner all her "negativity." This caused her to fear that her boyfriend would leave her – after all, neither her "perfection" nor her "negativity" were authentic – and she would become highly anxious, watching as if from a distance as she grew emotionally numb.

The next step was always the same: the person in the relationship would begin to complain about Elaine's aloofness and her desire to control. The damage to Elaine was so massive, as a result of a childhood full of pain, that even when she understood that she was afraid and that the numbness was defensive, this pattern still dictated the direction of each relationship.

Elaine's childhood was filled with unrelenting fear, anxiety, and humiliation. She felt her only recourse was to try to ward off the blows that related not to her own behavior, but to her mother's internal state. She had no control whatsoever over what happened in the home. In fact, she became convinced that her behavior had no effect whatsoever on her world. Her need to be in control made it very difficult for her to process her experience, and yet she had to if she wanted to advance emotionally. Furthermore, her mother was still alive, and continued to say terrible things to her in their weekly conversations.

It took all of Elaine's trust and courage to let herself review and process her life. Little by little she told her story and allowed herself to re-experience the awful childhood she had lived through. She remembered having had attachments, then having them taken away from her; this helped her to see that her ability to attach had once been very normal, though it had diminished when under attack. Though it was a slow process for Elaine, she came to remember the good times with her father, her excitement over her gifts, and her attachment to specific toys that were then taken from her. She let herself re-experience the joy of attachment, even though, in her case, remembering the *happiness* necessitated remembering *loss* as well. She came to see that to recover her feelings, to open the door to new experiences, she would have to accept some sad ones.

Denying these early experiences, and keeping their memory at bay, had permitted them to gain an inordinate degree of power over her. Upon examination, these memories, while sad, no longer had the ability to terrorize Elaine. On working through those early experiences, Elaine gained the ability to move beyond them, to arrive at an emotional state that had been her developmental birthright, but which had been thwarted by emotional trauma. It is never too late to advance to the next developmental milestone – all it takes is the willingness to provide the self-nurturing and acceptance you so desperately need.

Elaine also stopped making excuses for her mother, whom she really did see as more bad than good. She put limits on their conversations, and eventually needed to stop speaking to her altogether. Her father had been kind to the children in his own interactions with them, but had not protected them. He still defended the mother, even though they had been divorced for some time. Elaine had idealized her father as the nice parent, because her mother had been so bad, but she now had to remove her father from the pedestal of idealization she had placed him on. He was, in fact, angry with Elaine because she needed to stop speaking to her mother – not out of malice, but simply because she couldn't recover unless she did so.

While Elaine had definite issues with her father, as his faults had been quite serious, she decided that she still loved him enough to try to mend their relationship. She had a talk with her father in which she told him he hadn't protected her and was still acting like her feelings didn't matter, and that he now had a chance to show her that they did. Luckily for Elaine – and it was certainly about time – her father apologized and said he would discuss this over time with her whenever she needed to. He told her about his own childhood and described his own guilt over his mentally-ill mother. He took responsibility for doing the wrong thing, and said that Elaine's coming to him was helping him resolve his own feelings that had not mattered much to him either.

With this new support from her father, things got a bit easier for Elaine. She acknowledged her attachment to him, and at last felt confident that he was not going to abandon her. She had not known this before speaking to him, and had been genuinely afraid that her father would not have anything to do with her if she continued not to speak to her mother. Elaine would have done what she needed to regardless of her father's response, but I was glad for her that something had been salvaged. He became instrumental in her healing, and agreed to share in her sad story. Elaine came to realize that if her father *had* ended his relationship with her, it would have meant that he didn't love her. Now she saw that he did, even though he had seriously neglected his parental responsibilities. His regret made up for a great deal of the hurt this had caused Elaine.

In her relationships, Elaine needed to know plans in advance down to the last detail, and she was very controlling. She could not let herself get attached to jobs, and went from one to the other without any long-term plans for the future. She tried to control everything, which caused her to become anxious and leave. Elaine came to value her ability to attach and to tolerate her sad feelings, and she became better able to accept that what she dreaded and tried to control – sudden loss – had already happened.

Elaine came to realize she could only control herself. This awareness made her much stronger. She finally found a job and an apartment she loved, and discovered that she no longer felt numb when she made a new friend or dated a new person. She was much better. She had come to me with depression and an anxiety disorder, as she was anxious whenever she couldn't control everything. Her path was a long one, but the anxiety was the first symptom to disappear. When she realized that she could only control herself, she decided to live life fully, to love with a full heart, and let others do what they were going to do. She decided to have as much control over her own life as possible, by making good decisions and living fully. Ironically, letting go of controlling others gives you more control over *yourself* and your *own* life – where control belongs.

The urge to control everything and to eliminate surprises comes from a time when just the opposite was true. "Susan" was given almost no choices by her rigid, domineering parents. Her parents chose her friends and activities. They later even chose her electives when she was in high school. Her mother decided how she was to wear her hair and which clothes she was to wear. If there had ever been a time Susan argued or tried to assert her own will, it was long forgotten, and she felt that she didn't even have a will of her own. Ironically, she tried to control events and people, but with respect to her own life she asked nothing.

Susan was very depressed and didn't know why, but she had little pleasure in life. She began to see her life as just going forward without her having much to do about it. She began to obsess about a friend who had tragically shot himself many years before. She saw this as a loss of control and was terrified for herself. I told her that the decision to shoot oneself was not the result of a loss of control, but represented a sad planning of events, and a determination that *did* require much control in a very tragic way.

I asked Susan if she thought she could somehow lose control of herself, go into a kind of trance-like state, and shoot herself. She said yes, she felt that she could. She felt so little control in her life that she imagined that the act of committing suicide was the result of the complete loss of control of both body and mind. This belief, which of course had no basis in reality, gives some idea of the terrible inner state in which Susan lived. She saw the absurdity of this, but said that she was afraid of doing things and not knowing what she was doing – in other words, acting from a total loss of control. This potential loss of control represented a portion of Susan's Abyss.

Because her childhood experience trained her to please others, Susan had learned to numb herself to her own desires. She had no access to her hopes and fears, and this lack of awareness of her own innermost feelings led to the development of the Abyss within Susan. What she feared most *was* the fear itself – as is often the case when examining the contents of one's Abyss. She became much less anxious and depressed as she took more control over her life, and was more and more honest with herself. Over time, she recognized the underlying suicidal ideation, and she was happy to claim her life and her decisions. She forgave her parents for trying to live her life for her, and was determined never to let it happen again.

Susan felt no control in her life at all, felt there were no choices for her, and was afraid to face what made her so afraid. She did not want to go on living this way. Her only goal was to try to please, and she was terrified of her hatred of her life. It was a happy day for both of us when she was able to take some control over her life and enjoy it. When she began to honor her own feelings and needs, she knew she had come more fully into her authentic self. Remember, controlling yourself and your decisions about your life is healthy, but you cannot control anyone else. Susan's parents had made her feel she had no choices at all and that there was no control or pleasure in life. Her Abyss, the way she was made to feel, was of not being alive. When her despair became too much to bear, it is no wonder that she focused on her friend's suicide.

The strong desire for control and predictability also relates to perfectionism and shame. If you feel you need to be perfect and live in dread of shame, you will not welcome situations in which you need to be more spontaneous.

"Helen" became very anxious when she couldn't fully plan things in advance, even when she couldn't plan a vacation down to the last detail. If she and her husband scheduled in "free time," what if she didn't have the right thing to wear, for example? She felt that when predictability was lacking, mistakes were just waiting to happen, which caused her severe anxiety. Depending on the kind of childhood people have had, control and predictability represent an attempt to avoid shame, humiliation, and mistreatment. Though it is scary and painful, facing the unknown must be done. What a loss to have to forgo any excitement at all just to keep avoiding real or imagined emotional blows! There is a much better way to live.

On a more underlying level, we can say that people who have PCS dynamics are afraid of being in situations in which they cannot strongly censor themselves. Conversely, in those who stringently censor themselves, but who are unconsciously attracted to loosening their inhibitions, a desire to drink alcohol or to smoke pot may be overwhelming. Such a person might feel inadequate in social settings *without* this artificial "loosener."

If the need to censor, or the fear of losing one's inhibitions, is strong enough, it could lead to very rigid standards about drugs and alcohol, since drinking causes a person to lose their inhibitions. In every-day life situations, they do not trust themselves to respond appropriately if they cannot foresee every detail of what is coming. Dreading making a mistake of any kind or a lack of predictability seems perilous. Life has taught many people that they could be shamed or punished at any time for any reason, and a major force in their lives is to avoid this at all costs.

When underlying issues are faced and resolved, the desire to control everything melts away. Internal order and a sense of safety replace the need to perfectly order all the externals. The idea that you can control others by trying to be perfect for them is replaced by simply trying to do your best. You can come to see that you might have choices you did not anticipate, but that not all of them are life-changing or important. It is not all-or-nothing, as we discussed in the chapter on rigidity and black-and-white thinking. It is important to remember that the most dreaded fears are of things that have already happened.

I have seen many PCS people agonize over planning a wedding, which even non-PCS often do. I myself had a small wedding with thirty people. Because my husband and I had had friends that differed widely from each other, politically and in other ways, we had a careful seating arrangement so that people we thought could not get along wouldn't be next to each other. It turned out that the arrangements got all mixed up and the seating was exactly what we had tried to avoid. When we first saw this we were horrified, but it turned out that everyone not only got along, but also had a good time. It was ironic that the detail we really anguished over was the one that was ruined, and a good time was had by all. It's a good rule in life to "expect the unexpected," and often the unexpected works out for the best.

A final topic that belongs in this chapter is the PCS person's possessiveness about their things. Many clients have told me that since they could never rely on people, a beloved stuffed animal, picture, or souvenir became very important, representing the significant person with whom they really yearned to have the stable relationship. This object offered comfort, safety, and support in a way their loved ones could not always do.

While it is common and normal for young children to have these transitional objects to maintain a connection to their mother when they are separated, adults also do this when they were never able to internalize a good, strong sense of security in their important relationships. For these adults, any change or loss in the physical environment represents a severe lack of control and a loss of the valued relationship or lifestyle. This terror is very real.

"Sandy" and her husband were planning to move out-of-state, and she was absolutely terrified. Her home, representing her marriage, was about to be left behind. Compounding matters, they had to live in temporary housing for a few months in order to find an appropriate home and learn about their new location.

This was the Abyss: Sandy's unstable family moved frequently, leaving friends and relatives behind, sometimes for years, and she feared falling into the chaos she had grown up in. Sandy said she felt no control whatsoever, and felt as though she were stepping off into the darkness. The predictability was gone. The familiar home with all its things would not be there to remind Sandy everything was okay. This move represented a step into the unknown.

Sandy knew that she really did want to make the move, and she understood her dynamics. With the courage she had always shown, she went with her husband, knowing that she had to cross over this bridge of fear. Her desire for new adventures was stronger than her fear.

You have seen in this chapter how people who fear the unpredictable because of their early experiences are in reality afraid of a new circumstance freeing an aspect of their personality they feel they must control. Their attempts to control their lives leave no room for the unknown or serendipitous, which can enrich the lives of those without this fear. It can lead to a life of rigid rules and even rituals, as well as associated spokes of the PCS constellation of traits. I hope you have gained some consolation and courage from the stories of my clients who have freed themselves from the need to impose their control over external events and people, and who in the process have gained more true control by being aware of their deeper feelings and motivations.

Exercises

The following exercises are designed to help you look under your desire to control, and examine what it is you fear. Which of those fears belong to the past?

Exercise

What things do you wake up to and see throughout the day that give you comfort and let you know things are all right in your life? What do they represent for you?

Exercise 2

Think of an instance in which you were told you over-planned and over-controlled. What were you afraid would happen if you did not do this? Did you think you would be blamed or held responsible in some way if things went wrong?

Exercise 3

What does change represent to you? Write out a fantasy change and what that would mean to you.

Exercise 4

Think of and write down a few losses in your life, even if they were the result of normal growth, such as leaving home to go to school. Were you able to grieve as you welcomed in the new situation?

Chapter 7

Decision-Making

Before we get into how difficult making decisions probably is for you, we need to think about Melanie Klein's developmental theory, which we discussed in Chapter 5. This is not really a book about theory, so we will just be covering the parts relevant to your own understanding and emotional progress.

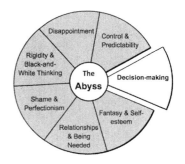

Remember that in Klein's theory there are two main developmental stages. The beauty of her theory is that she covers so many areas with just those two stages. For Klein, the first stage of development involves splitting and projective identification. This may be easier to understand if you think of small children you know. When is the last time you saw one who did not think in terms of black-and-white and all-good and all-bad, and who took responsibility for his actions? It doesn't happen very often, because it really isn't supposed to. Instead, small children use projection and projective identification in their interactions with the world.

In projection, one attributes a feeling to someone else. A feeling of dissatisfaction with what one has done becomes a fear that someone will criticize it. In the mother-child relationship, we often call the mother, the target of the projection, a "container," allowing the young child to disavow strong feelings until such time in development as they can be owned. When a small child is told that it is bedtime, he or she often tells the mother she is mean, and a good-enough mother just accepts this, the projection of the child's anger.

Developmentally, projective identification is a normal and necessary process in which the child projects feelings onto the mother, and takes the combination of her own responses and those projections in, which is called introjection. An angry child will see himself and the mother as worse and worse, and a contented one will see herself and the mother as better and better. When a mother responds without inordinate anger of her own, the child's will dissipate and self and others will seem calmer and more content. You can think of containing feelings as letting someone take them out on you, as is appropriate with a very young child.

In the first stage, we think of an infant, although in our society there are few who even get through this stage successfully, as Winnicott said. The child splits and experiences everything as all-good or all-bad. There are no gray areas, no ambivalence. In Klein's ideal stages (which are not always the way things turn out), the infant is supposed to discover early on that the mother who satisfies and protects is also the one who angers and frustrates – after all, even the best mother is not perfect.

When the mother is perceived as good, the child perceives himself as good; when the mother is bad, the child perceives himself as bad. He projects his feelings onto the mother, then takes them back in, and this cycle constantly reinforces and heightens the infant's feelings about himself. When the mother is disturbed, the child feels badly about her – and himself. He lacks the capacity to conceive of himself as a separate entity, or to recognize that it could be possible to be good even though the mother might not be. When the mother is attentive and nurturing, it is to the infant's benefit that he finds the mother to be a part of him. His self-image is developing along normal, healthy lines, and the feelings he projects onto the mother, then takes back in, teach him that he is good.

Because the infant, in the normal course, will always have angry feelings (when he is waiting for a feeding, a diaper change, etc.), the mother's job is to contain these feelings for the infant. When his cries are answered by her soothing touch, he is then able to feel that she has transformed his anger into something gentle and warm, and also he will not believe that he has injured her with his anger. This is very important, because if she were to respond in anger, he *would* believe that his angry feelings had actually hurt her.

When the baby's cries frustrate and anger the mother, the infant now has two sets of anger to contend with – his own, and the mother's. Now, instead of feeling that a softening presence has tempered his own anger, the infant takes in his mother's anger in addition to his own; nothing has soothed his original anger. Not only does his own anger grow, but he also believes he has hurt his mother. And in response, he feels that she now wants to hurt him, to retaliate. If this becomes a cycle, it can be very damaging to the infant's emotional growth.

Although we cannot remember our infancies, we can tell from later memories when mothers have not been able to contain the feelings of their children and, in fact, have blamed them for being helpless and needy; this has devastating effects. This is the point that most confuses people. I can't count the number of times I have heard someone say that if we can't remember infancy, then it can't have had any lasting impact on us, for good or for bad. In order to understand how something we don't remember can have long-term consequences in our lives, it helps to remember *context*.

When we witness a mother with her infant, we understand what is going on. The mother has brought this child into the world, and it is now her responsibility to meet his needs. If he cries, we know it is her job to calm him and to provide him with nourishment and comfort. But the infant doesn't "know" anything. Each moment of his life he is being "taught" what he is, what his mother is, and what life is all about, by his mother's responses to him. He doesn't know that he is supposed to count on her for everything; what he knows is what he in fact experiences. And each moment with the mother teaches him a bit more about himself and about the world.

These messages can permanently affect the way he views the world throughout his life, as they are his introduction to the world. For the rest of his life, the *context* for all of his later experiences will be the way he was cared for by his mother when he was "new" in this world. He may not remember those interactions, but his perceptions of the world will have grown from out of those early interactions.

If you traveled to a foreign country, and were given a kiss on each cheek by every stranger you met, you would begin to develop an opinion about the people in that country. You might tell a friend, "People over there are very friendly and are always kissing and touching." They would have provided you with a context for understanding their culture.

It is similar for an infant. He decides the world is a certain way, all based upon the way his mother is. So just imagine what sort of impact this has when the mother responds to his cries with frustration and anger, or when she ignores his cries altogether. What sorts of ideas would the infant begin to develop about this world?

Klein tells us that when the world (and after all, what is *the world* to a child?) is more good than bad, the child will have the strength to stop splitting, or thinking in black-and-white terms. He will begin to move toward the next stage of development, involving integration, which is the goal of therapy in my view. The young child realizes that the good mother is the same person as the bad one – what a letdown! And yet it is so much healthier – because it is a response to actual reality – for the infant to get to this place in his understanding. If he were to keep the perfect, idealized mother separated in his mind, and imagine that another, demonized mother existed alongside of her, what sorts of ramifications would there be for people who entered into his life at a later stage? What would the ramifications be for the way this child viewed his own shortcomings and faults? If the child tucks away the parts of himself he dislikes, and denies they exist, he may create a hidden place deep inside of himself to contain those ideas and feelings. As he ages, these feelings and ideas develop more fully into his own, unique Abyss.

You can see why it is important to move to an integrated view of things, and to accept that you are the same person all the time, however angry or disappointed you may sometimes feel. As for others, you also need to recognize that the same person who angers or annoys you is the person whose company you greatly enjoy. There is no need to keep the two polarized personalities separated, and at such extreme ends of your understanding of yourself and others.

Recall the young woman from a previous chapter who realized that she and others are not perfect. Yes, this is healthier, but this step involves some sadness and pain. The child realizes that there is just one mother, that she is mostly good, but that she is far from perfect. When there is more good than bad, this can be faced with courage, and that brings the end of perfectionism and black-and-white thinking. If development does not occur normally, one must do this work in therapy or by working on oneself.

What happens when there is not more good than bad? I used to do psychological evaluations for the child welfare system, and tested many children of all ages in foster care, who had been abused, neglected, and had mothers who didn't see them regularly. Certainly they knew that they didn't come first in the mothers' lives – far from it. While these children were almost always in conflict with other mother figures, such as foster parents, they were extremely protective of their birth mothers! They would totally change the story of how they had come into foster care, so that in their new versions of the story, their mother was innocent, and they would split off their resentment and project it onto other mother figures. Their birth mothers were preserved as all-good and the replacement mothers became all-bad. The children "got rid of" their painful feelings, and held onto their denial, by demonizing these new mothers, though they were not the ones who had hurt them.

Thus, the good-mother fantasy was preserved – but now these children found themselves at odds with their foster parents, teachers, caseworkers, and the rest of the adult world. In other words, those who provided help were hated for it. What a high price to pay to keep their idealized mother!

These children's worlds were not experienced as more good than bad, and they continued to use splitting. One girl whose siblings, like herself, were all sexually abused by one or another of the mother's partners, dwelled on what a pretty voice her mother had when she sang, and how her mother was "so nice", even though they were all in foster care and had suffered so very much. The legacy left to her was that, in her attempt to idealize a very confused and inadequate mother, she could not love anyone else, not even someone who might be capable of caring for her and loving her back.

We see this with adults, too. For people who follow Melanie Klein, idealization is always a sign of splitting and of hiding from the negative. Adults who have positive relationships with their parents can say jokingly how they perhaps "drive each other crazy" about something or other, and this is not a threatening thing to them. Then there are adults who say their parents were "wonderful," and in fact had no faults at all. These are people who are too frightened to put their parents to the more-good-than-bad test, because they are afraid their parents will not pass it and they are afraid to face the pain. As this type of person grows older, the all-good/all-bad or black-and-white thinking may extend into other areas.

Additionally, just as we have seen with the abused children I used to work with, many people who do this will be extremely critical of others. Insisting on a perfect mental picture of the mother, other people get blamed for feelings that really were meant for the mother. Thus, we see many adults who have problems with those in authority and who are angered by any real or imagined slight, and adults never want to contain the feelings of other adults.

Another part of Klein's second stage is the idea of making reparations. Klein said that the very young child feels her anger has hurt the mother, and she then tries to fix her, or to atone. People with PCS anxieties often try to repair others and feel terrible if they cannot. Maybe you have tried to help others, only to find that they rejected your advice or did not show appropriate gratitude. Some people are stuck in this second stage in part because they cannot stop making reparations.

I believe perfectionism is, among other things, an attempt to repair imagined damage, and if something remains imperfect, how can the perfectionist's efforts serve as atonement? Can you think of significant early people in your life that you have tried to fix or repair? It is well known that people cannot repair parents or people who are too close. In your own recovery from PCS anxieties, it is very important to face times when you felt angry with a parent, and to acknowledge the guilt that this produced. People who are "rescuers" are unconsciously doing atonement or making reparations, and unless the real issues are faced, it just doesn't work.

As a psychologist, I very often see this kind of guilt. A young teacher said that his mother had been on the verge of a writing career when he was born, and he blamed himself for her not following her dream. Of course, his mother went on to give birth to his younger brother. Another young person told me that her mother had gone to college and could have had a scholarship to graduate school, but became pregnant, and because she did the "responsible thing" she "lost everything." She never quite had it, but lost it. By the way, there is nothing – and I mean *nothing* – responsible about making a child feel guilty because you chose to have him instead of pursuing a career you want to pretend you would have had. How much easier it is to say we would have been great were it not for someone else, than to try to achieve something!

"Tami" was a parentified child whose mother made herself sound like a martyr for having to work while her young child took care of the household. When her mother wanted to go out, she would say, "With all I have to do for you I need a night out once in a while."

It is not hard to see where these mothers were coming from, but doing this to a child is especially toxic. Even if a child manages to get through the first stage without feeling his or her anger has harmed the mother, internalizing this toxicity causes the child to believe that he or she really *did* do irreparable damage to the mother.

I don't know if you have ever felt that you have damaged your mother by angry thoughts, and I don't know if your mother made you feel responsible because she didn't have a career – one she wanted to think would have been brilliant. But I know how hard it is to take responsibility for your own feelings and actions if your mother did not do so herself, and made you feel responsible for the world that she created. No child should be made to feel this way.

Are you the type of person who thinks you have to make reparations or atone for something you didn't do, or to try to fix something or someone? If so, it is essential that you honestly look at these dynamics. You can no longer be responsible for the choices others have made when you were barely conceived. Your mother has her own dynamics and her own reasons for not taking responsibility, and it is time for you to stop carrying the load and life lessons of another. Maybe your mother never did lay blame on you for her decisions, but she presents as vulnerable, and you feel you must fix her. Again, you can't. It is sad and difficult to love someone with psychological problems, and this makes it all the more important to have good personal boundaries.

Kevin, a client I talked about in chapter 5, said that his mother, who is divorced and never remarried, behaves in a masochistic manner with men, with each decision worse than the next. Kevin gives his mother advice and tries to "fix" her, which of course doesn't work. Kevin has tried for years to make these kinds of reparations, as he was blamed by his mother for the custody arrangement imposed on him, as well as for his relationship with his father. It is so intensely burdensome for a child to be blamed for something for which he has absolutely no responsibility, and all the more so when it is something the adults imposed on *him*. Yet, Kevin grew up with this blame. I cannot stress this enough: there are few things more painful for a child than to be made to feel responsible for things he has *no* control over. Is it any wonder that the need for control can become so pervasive in such a person?

Kevin has walked a very long path in therapy. In a recent visit with his mother, he became angry when she kept talking about her dysfunctional relationships with men. Making matters worse, the mother misinterpreted his anger and frustration as meaning that he somehow didn't care; her immaturity and selfishness prevented her from seeing her child's needs, just like when he was growing up. He lashed out, and rightfully so, telling her that all through his childhood she had told him these things and was still doing it and not changing. The mother got very angry and exaggerated what he had said. She told him she wouldn't bring *anything* up with him ever again, since he wasn't interested.

The very positive aspect of this is that Kevin no longer wants to be used. He no longer sets out to "prove" to himself who he is or isn't according to his interaction with his mother. The mistake he made – an understandable one since this is the first time he is setting boundaries and will need some experience to see what works – was to point out to his mother that she was behaving selfishly, had hurt him in the past, and was still hurting him. It was of course extremely painful for Kevin to see what little effect this had. What he will need to do is tell his mother that certain topics are off limits, that they upset him, and that they will need to have a relationship that omits topics that cause him so much pain.

Every adult has the right and the need to set personal boundaries. With all the progress Kevin has made, I suspect that he is ready to see he cannot fix his mother, even though she keeps provoking him into trying. It is an old, tired dance, and it is not malicious or uncaring to refuse to do it, as it is unhealthy for his mother to want him to be a witness to her self-harming behavior. It is like when she blamed him in the past for visiting with his father and stepmother; now she is blaming him for not fixing her, but she does not really want to change or she would get help.

Kevin is close to saying something like, "You are my mother and I love you, but it is very upsetting to me to hear about behavior where you set yourself up to be mistreated, and I need to not talk about those things anymore. I hope you can respect this and my feelings, and if you start I will remind you that we need to change the subject." Kevin hopes that he can still have a relationship with his mother – a healthier one – but he is prepared to take a break from it if no limits are accepted. He knows that caring about someone doesn't mean letting them treat you however they want to.

Remember, we don't fix anyone; people fix themselves. In therapy you have someone who knows your dynamics, cares about you, and walks the path with you – but *you* are the one changing and doing the work. People have to want help to change, and when they just want to enmesh you in dysfunctional behavior, they are not really asking for help.

You can see that when children are made to feel they are at fault for things totally outside of their control, any decisions they make take on mammoth proportions. They so badly want to do the right thing, and know all too well what can happen as a result of bad decisions. All decisions are so emotionally loaded.

"Candice" was a young professional woman who was very poised on the outside, but who suffered from depression and was almost immobilized when she had to make decisions. Her mother divorced her father when she was very young, and remarried a very disturbed man. The mother was extremely passive, and told Candice when she was very small that the stepfather supported them, and that they couldn't do anything to "make him mad" or they would be in a horrible situation.

Candice lived at the mercy of this man's decisions. He would get into altercations with the neighbors, resulting in frequent moves. She attended at least two new schools each year, either because of these moves or because he would "decide" that a school was no longer appropriate, which was very hard for her. The stepfather would fly into scary rages if she had a friend over, so the mother told her to stop. He would suddenly "decide" that a television show was inappropriate in the middle of her watching something. Every time he would decide something it would be to her detriment. He would get uncontrollably angry for tiny things, such as when she forgot to say "please" when asking for something.

When her stepfather would go into a rage, she would always be blamed. Now that Candice is an adult, her mother idealizes her childhood, and the mother's own mental health has deteriorated. While Candice is very likeable and bright, she agonized over decisions, so afraid she would somehow cause something devastating to happen.

What happens to people when they are made to feel at fault for the decisions of others? When they are made to feel they are so powerful that the weight of the world is on their shoulders? That they need to fix those who raised them, and should have done things right for them? One thing that happens is that decisions are never neutral: they are earth-shattering. One possible choice is somehow good, and the other is seen as potentially devastating.

Remember, if you think everything is your fault, and that you are that powerful, each and every decision leads to huge imaginary consequences. Here we have not only the black-and-white thinking, but also the guilt and desire to repair. Each decision weighs so very heavily, even when it is not such a big one.

The truth is, whatever we do is imperfect. Whether you select choice A or choice B, there will be pros and cons to either one. This is not unique to you, but is true for all of us.

One thing I'd like you to think about is what I call "morally-neutral territory." Recall the client who always expressed guilt when she hadn't cleaned her apartment. Whether or not to clean her apartment was a decision that affected only her, as she lived alone. She alone would have to live in a dirty apartment, but would also have had the extra free time not cleaning would have afforded her. The decision to clean or not to clean is morally-neutral and has nothing to do with whether she is a good person. However, this was a long and painful realization for her, as her parents always treated morally-neutral ground the same way they treated clearly moral issues. Not cleaning one's apartment doesn't rank with slandering someone, after all.

"Judith" and her husband were in the process of buying a house. One was a little less expensive but needed some fixing-up; the other cost more but was fine as is. She went back and forth repeatedly, agonizing over this decision, which affected both her sleep and nearly every waking minute. Her husband didn't care which house they bought and thought both were nice, that there were pros and cons to each.

When she was able to process this, she expressed her fear that her parents would criticize her decision, and we worked on Judith recognizing that she only had responsibility for her own life. She could either agree with her parents or say the topic was now off limits. The house that needed some work was basically in good condition, so we are not talking about buying a major fixer-upper. She said that her parents would probably emphasize all the work to be done and the trouble it would be, or they could emphasize the high cost of the other house.

You can see what was really at stake here: Judith had grown up in the belief that not only could *she* never make the right decision, but that there was somehow a third decision that her *parents* would have gotten right. When both choices had their own pros and cons, all Judith could have done would have been to decide which of the two made the most sense for her.

Judith's whole life had been like this, and it is no wonder she always felt she had to make the "perfect" decision. She eventually had to see that her parents always blamed her for their own shortcomings, real or imagined. While this work was not fast or easy, nor was it possible for this issue to be worked through in time for buying the house to be less stressful, her anxiety over this decision was the impetus that brought her to therapy. The push to the Abyss was making a "bad" decision, and the Abyss itself was being stupid and "spacey" – as her parents always told her she was.

Judith finally reached the point where she understood that this was how her parents felt about themselves, and where she knew she had to put limits on the way they treated her. As an adult living a responsible life with her husband and children, it was inappropriate for her parents to reprimand her for any decision she made.

The other source of pain in deciding which house to buy was that Judith enjoyed rehabbing; after all, this is like making reparations, isn't it? Taking something in need of repair and fixing it was almost like an offering to her parents for all the disappointment they were determined to feel in her. Yet, she really wanted the house that didn't need any work. The mortgage payments would not be that much higher and, as she put it, "For once I want something that is fine as is." *For once.* She was exhausted from having tried to fix people all her life and weighing her own self-evaluation in terms of what her parents said, which was a losing battle. She was tired of trying to repair people, and rehabbing a house felt too much like that to her. There was no "perfect" offering she could ever make to her parents.

Judith came to see that her parents were determined to be disappointed in her and in themselves. They were disappointed in everything, after all. She reached a point at which she decided she preferred having a relationship with her parents to not having one, but no longer wanted to be treated this way. I told her that adults do put limits on what they do and do not want to hear or talk about.

She finally told her parents that if they wanted to be disappointed in her, even though she was a good and responsible person, that was their right, but it was her right not to want to hear it in direct or indirect ways. She said that it would take time to change, but she was not going to ask their opinions about everything. If they wanted a relationship with her, they could have it, but only if there was mutual respect. The way this worked out was that, after saying a few times how "touchy" she had become – to which she agreed, replying, "I know I am, and I don't want to hear one negative thing about myself" – her parents decided that they could live within the limits.

When one parent would test the waters, the way a small child would do, Judith understood that her parents were very similar to children. She would laughingly remind them they were testing and tell them to back off, which they would do. It might not have worked out this way – and she was prepared for this possibility – but Judith knew she had to grow to respect herself and to make others respect her. As she worked on these issues, it became easier and easier to admit to herself and to others when she was wrong, because she allowed herself to just be human.

Which house did Judith and her husband buy? Well, they bought the one for a little more money that did not need fixing-up. She felt a little guilty about this, but did it anyway, confident now in herself and her therapy. She is now living a happy and peaceful life, having had the courage to face her own anxieties and insecurities. Ultimately, purchasing the house she didn't have to fix up was a liberating act, symbolizing that she was finished with trying to fix her parents. Most importantly, her decisions were now her own.

An issue that did come up, of course, was facing the fact that her parents were not really acting out of what was best for her, but could not tolerate any imperfection in themselves or someone they saw as an extension of themselves. Judith would say over and over to them, "I'm me, you're you," and this was probably very therapeutic for them. Her mother once told her that she handled a situation with a friend the same way, and had learned that others have their own Self as well, a huge step for her.

"Lindsey" came in for her first session wearing a very pretty sweater. She looked so nice in it I had to compliment her. She burst out crying and said her mother did not like that color – and she was in her 30s! Going shopping (talk about a morally-neutral area!) was extremely stressful to her with all the decisions it entailed, because her mother and her criticisms were in her head constantly. Her mother was quite disturbed and tried to own all aspects of her children's lives, even telling her children that they should always tell her every single thing they were thinking. In spite of having this psychologically-dangerous mother, this client was able to use her superior intelligence and courage to work through all of the issues leading to her anxieties, learning to set limits, and even stand up to her siblings to be her own person. While at first Lindsay just wanted her mother to approve of her, she did let go of this, and her decisions became her own, rather than a battleground for her and her mother.

In looking at your difficulty in making decisions, what is it you are afraid of? Certainly, decision-making, or making the "wrong" decision, can nudge you toward the Abyss.

What is *your* Abyss? How were you portrayed when you didn't do exactly as your parents wanted? Do your decisions involve making reparations? Do all your decisions make you either a good or bad person? Is any one decision all-good or all-bad? Or is it something that should be neutral? What criticisms are you afraid of hearing in your head, and perhaps in reality? What are you afraid of facing in your parents that impedes your ability to decide? Are you ready to have an autonomous self?

When parents have been basically good, they are owed some degree of respect, empathy, and dignity. If your parents provided a decent home, maybe you owe it to them not to become a criminal or bring disgrace on everyone, just as you owe this to yourself.

Yet, parents are supposed to nurture you, the Self that they brought into this world. It was never intended that they should own that Self. Parents do not have the right to choose someone's career. Yes, they might want to identify with someone, living out a secret wish of their own, but it is not the child's function to fulfill this fantasy for them. Parents do not get to have children simply so that they can live vicariously through them.

If you are a decent person, you should be loved as you are, and if you are not allowed to have a real Self, you are paying too high a price. What if you hate your job and your parents suggest you find another one before quitting? Well, that is good advice, and you should know that yourself anyway. But what if they say it is such a noble career, they hate to see you change? Or that what you would like to do instead simply isn't as good? That is overstepping. You can learn to know the difference, and to finally decide for yourself.

Exercises

In this chapter we have looked at why decision-making can be such an emotionally-loaded issue. We have looked at different events and issues that make a decision much more than what it really is.

Clearly, for PCS people there is a unique Abyss – something that a "wrong" decision represents and that can be quite painful. The following exercises are designed to take you closer to what this might be.

Exercise 1

Think about a few decisions that have been hard for you to make. Think about some you made that involved big sacrifices that didn't need to be made, such as doing something for your child who needed you. Jot down a few decisions you have made, the guilt and anxiety both sides of the decisions presented to you, and what the Abyss was in each case. What kind of horrible person were you made to feel yourself to be if you didn't do everything someone else's way? This brings you closer to the Abyss. Look beneath the surface and remember you have the right to be your own person.

Exercise 2

Were you ever made to feel guilty or responsible for someone else's decisions? Who was it? Who said they made a particular decision because of you, when you had no say in the matter? How have you felt that your gratitude for this so-called favor needed to be expressed? Write out your answers in your journal.

Exercise 3

Write about a time when you were abused, shamed, belittled, etc. What was said to you? Note how you feel and remember that you are an adult now and have no one to answer to. Do some deep breathing. Now imagine yourself as the adult you are today, and imagine a small child in the situation you were in. Behave appropriately toward that child. In this way you can repair yourself.

Exercise 4

Do you feel responsible for things now that simply aren't your responsibility? Which things? Make a list and try to determine why you feel responsible. Try to distinguish between past and present, and see that what you fear has already happened. The more you confront the past, the less you will fear criticism for your decisions in the present.

Exercise 5

Can you think of some decisions that were hard for you to make? What were you afraid would happen? Did you feel you would be shamed, judged, or that you might disappoint someone? How were you afraid of feeling?

Now think of an imaginary situation that is similar, and in your mind face the situation. Can you handle the feelings? What mental dialogue will you use to do what *you* feel is right?

Exercise 6

Write down several examples of times when you were afraid to make a decision because of self-judging. Go back in your mind and see what your associations were in connection with these decisions. Has anything changed in terms of the strength of the associations? Are they weaker now?

Exercise 7

Engage in deep breathing and recall a very recent decision, or one that is coming up that involves a lot of anxiety. Try to see what you are really afraid of. Use your adult dignity and what you have learned to look at those fears and try to reason through each one.

Chapter 8

Fantasy & Self-Esteem

Why does this book include a chapter on fantasy? Well, fantasy is very important, and PCS types of people often have difficulty fantasizing. Fantasies can help us resolve difficulties, can inspire us, and can help us learn from generalized information without going through the exact experience. Fantasy also provides us with comfort, motivation, and inspiration.

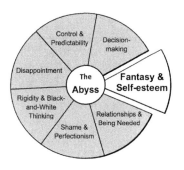

So many clients tell me that they can't decide which career they want to follow. Yes, it's a decision – and you have seen how much trouble PCS people have making decisions – but still, why do people tell me they don't know if they would like something or not? Why can't they just put together what they know about themselves, what they like and don't like, and figure out if they would be happy in something without actually doing it? Yet this is what people tell me, and it is because they have difficulty fantasizing, or don't give enough importance or time to it. It is a significant deprivation in life to have little or no fantasy life, as it helps us know ourselves better and gives us a safe time and place for real feelings without acting them out. Perhaps most importantly, fantasies let us know things about ourselves and our preferences, without having to change anything to gain this knowledge.

People who cannot generalize their experience and use fantasy often say that they can only learn by doing something or being in a specific situation. We are not around that long! It is important to know yourself well enough not to have to go through each experience to learn things. People who hide from aspects of themselves, and fear disliking who they are, tend to avoid fantasy. Some immediately judge the fantasy, and some feel too shamed to even let themselves want something, even in fantasy.

One client told me she might want to be a teacher, and when I asked her if being with a group of children was something she would like, she said she had no idea. I asked if she knew any children, and she said she used to baby-sit on occasion and didn't like it. This was how out-of-touch she was with what she liked and wanted. Finally, she said that her mother was a teacher, and thought that teaching was a noble profession. As she talked about this, it was clear that she was afraid to want to be something her mother perhaps wouldn't think was so noble. It had not occurred to her to try to develop her own wishes. She was stuck because she didn't want to follow in her mother's footsteps, and yet felt that she should.

Another client always said that all she wanted was validation. She was a high school teacher and wasn't receiving validation from the adolescents she taught. Not surprisingly, she wanted to change her career. When I asked her what she wanted to do, she said she didn't care, as long as she was appreciated and treated well. I couldn't think of one job for which that is always the case. I asked her what she would like to do when she wakes up every day, and she said that she couldn't think beyond the validation.

I think sometimes the inability to decide what path to take in life has to do with wanting validation so badly that it is hard to use other information, and the lack of fantasy makes it even more difficult. This young adult was so unhappy with her self-evaluation that she couldn't even fantasize beyond just having some job that made her feel better about herself. She could not begin to think of what she would like, because the hunger for better self-esteem and wanting to feel worthy inhibited more productive fantasies. Another client said she would like to help people get organized, but just wanted grateful people – not people who didn't do what she wanted or who would disagree.

My clients always come in not really believing that change is possible. My hope is always that they can gain new insights immediately, realize that they are valuable, and remain invested in the process until the wonderful changes occur. However, it is not the job of the client to validate me. It is my job to help them achieve self-love, which reduces their need for so much validation. How could I help them reach that point if I needed validation from *them*?

Fantasy has certainly been important in my own life. When I was younger I would read books about therapy and knew I wanted to be a psychologist – and I do love it. I sometimes read about places I would like to visit, and fantasize about things I would like to do there. Then, when I do actually visit one of these places, I usually like it.

Some fantasies take the place of things we can really do, or give us ideas about things we would enjoy doing at a later time. Others involve things far outside the realm of possibility. For instance, we might fantasize about performing incredibly athletic feats when we are not at all athletic. I like to fantasize about being able to sing, because I really cannot, and I imagine the pleasure it would give someone to open their mouths and produce such wonderful sounds. Fantasy lets us not only make plans and see what we might or might not like, but can let us do a few things we really can't.

What do you fantasize or want to fantasize? Were you told day-dreaming was a waste of time? I am telling you the opposite. Nothing besides remembering and paying attention to your dreams puts you more in touch with yourself, your wishes, and your fears like a good fantasy. Do you fantasize about getting an apology from people who were unkind? From your parents? This is not a waste of time – far from it. These fantasies can then lead us to some good, strong decisions in reality. You might not ever get that apology, but maybe the fantasy will lead you to conclude it is time to start healing and living the life you want.

Some people feel a deep sense of shame over their fantasies. Really, why shouldn't you fantasize being President? Being an Olympic star? Being the boss of a large organization? I am not saying you should get stuck in fantasy, but that you should make friends with yours – with humor, compassion, strength, and insight.

When I was teaching child development at a college in Chicago, we discussed different personality types, how people have what we can call a God-given type, and then can be as balanced as possible within that type. For example, I wrote this book for your challenges, but what about people who are spontaneous, funny, fun-loving, and adventurous, who need to have more stability, responsibility, and consistency to achieve balance? We all have a life journey with lessons, and must try to achieve more insight and balance if we want that journey to make us wiser and better than we were when we started out.

During the period I was teaching, I was also doing psychological evaluations for children in foster care and knew a lot of caseworkers. I once said to my students, "If you are a good, fair, ethical person who cares about others, who likes telling others what to do, who enjoys being in charge, and who cares about child welfare, you might want to consider being a caseworker." I recounted how hard they worked supervising parents to see if they still had an abusive partner in the home, still used drugs, etc. One mother had angrily said, "[My caseworker] came to my house again and found my boyfriend there who I am not supposed to see 'cause of what he did to my kids, and she *liked* catching me!"

I asked her why that made her so angry. Given a job as caseworker, with low pay, having to protect other people's children, and seeing so many sad things, there should be something to like about the job. My students were embarrassed, saying that being "bossy" was not a good trait. Put into context, however, a good, ethical PCS type of person can make an outstanding caseworker, and would be fair and honest.

Fantasy is helpful because it gives you the chance to look at both the good and not-so-good aspects of your traits, and lets you think about where the more negative traits might be appropriate. One teacher laughingly told me how he once slipped up when an adult friend had cursed, and said, "NO! We don't use words like that!" While exerting some control in the classroom might be a good thing, and gave this teacher pleasure at the same time, it was a negative in his relationship with peers.

I do not like to control people, so being a therapist suits my personality. I like to connect and share my clients' feelings. I enjoy people becoming more and more aware and peaceful, and I like being a guide. But success or failure in therapy belongs to my clients. I know I do my part, but whether they do the work or not is up to them. After all, part of my job is helping people take responsibility for their lives, while creating more of the life they want and having compassion for themselves. Luckily for them and for me, my clients don't need much help with organization!

I strongly encourage you to let your fantasies develop. They are so very important – to your goals, to your sense of humor, to so very many things. Sometimes we can fantasize something we really wish we could do, leave the fantasy, make the goal a bit more realistic, and then set out to do it. But in any case, don't think that all of your thoughts have to be practical. What value is there in a human life without reflection, without wondering where we have been and where we wish to go? No matter what anyone has told you, I do hope you will become friends with your fantasies. You can then ask yourself why you might have those fantasies and use them to face your fears.

The topic of self-esteem appears in the same chapter as fantasy because how we think of ourselves has a lot to do with fantasy – our internal thinking. You do not want your whole inner life taken up with a dread of being imperfect, which only contributes to poor self-esteem and, put bluntly, takes you away from truly living. Enrich it with some healthy fantasy! You may be afraid of too much fantasy because of your fear of the Abyss, but I hope by now you are becoming more tolerant, compassionate, and aware of your real thoughts and feelings. Fantasy is a powerful tool in recovery.

You may have noticed that in this book I prefer to use the terms self-love or self-respect, rather than self-esteem. This is because I disagree with the emphasis our culture places on self-esteem, the push for achievement, and being better than others. In fact, the term "self-esteem" does imply being better than others in some way, making one person's feel-good solution another person's failure. According to most people's definition of self-esteem, only a small portion of the population could ever have an adequate amount. That can't be right, and we must be chasing after the wrong thing. Think about it. Only one person can get the highest grade in the class, be the best athlete, and be the best in any of our culturally-invented categories. I truly believe that being a good person, treating others decently, and trying to have meaningful work constitute a rich life. I do not think human worth is measured by one's grades, rank at work, looks, or the amount of money one has. I think one's character is what someone *is* – the rest are things that we *have*.

Some people try very hard to compensate for underlying feelings of unworthiness, but it is not really possible to counteract this through acquisitions. I cannot tell you how many people with PCS dynamics have come to me in crisis, having lost a job or failed a class. I am not saying that those are easy things to deal with. I *am* saying that one's feeling about oneself should not depend on these circumstances.

Likewise, extreme validation should be taken with a grain of salt and humility. When I was in psychoanalysis and idealized my analyst, he would laugh and reply that he was "only half as wonderful" as I thought. Teachers are often idealized, too. Years later, when I was teaching child development, students would sometimes tell me, often tearfully, what a "wonderful" person I was. For many of them, I was the first older person who treated them nicely and talked about *their* feelings. I would thank them, but repeat what my wise analyst told me. They never got to see my flaws, only the best of what I had to offer. We have all known a younger person who was impressed by a professor or someone higher up at their company, and who was all too quick to believe how "wonderful" the person was. Beware of put-downs and idealizations – both are false and passing.

If you lack self-worth, any blow at all, even an imagined blow, can be devastating, because it resonates with a feeling already there. I always tell my clients: People can only press a button if the button is there to begin with. I recall the tragic suicide of the father of my daughter's friend after he lost his job. His idea of himself was tied so closely to his job that without it he did not find a Self he thought was worthy. But we are not our jobs or our homes or our grades. Those are things we have, but they are not us and we are not them. In talking about self-esteem, most people are talking about having or doing more than others in some way. This is so sad and unhealthy, but it is so ingrained in our culture that it takes a great deal of effort to see on a deeper level than this.

An unfortunate aspect of PCS dynamics is that it causes people to harbor a feeling of being bad in some way, as we have touched on in every chapter. Whatever self-image you fear – whether it's being stupid, dishonest, angry, or lazy – when a situation comes along that seems to confirm it, the result is an emotional crisis. This is one reason it is often said that a crisis is a time of growth. When someone is in a crisis of this kind, you can give support and keep explaining how the situation doesn't mean what they think, but they won't believe you. Or, you can use the opportunity to find out what the Abyss means for the person, then help him see that there is a good, worthy self inside by encouraging him to face the false ideas he runs from. In this way, the person will not only recover from the crisis, but will begin to heal the chronic feelings from which he has always fled.

It is very important to know what you like and don't like about yourself. What would be the point of your life if you had nothing to work on at all? I am sixty years old now and have always worked on things about myself I'd like to change. This is a life-long endeavor. I strongly believe we are here to become better, more insightful, and more mature than we once were.

Without looking at yourself with a harsh eye, you should be aware of areas in which you are not strong. Maybe you are poor in math or have a bad sense of direction. Perhaps in relationships you need to feel needed but refuse to admit need, or maybe when you are with your parents you are prone to provoke arguments with them. Then look at your strengths. Perhaps you are very well-organized, like many of my friends with PCS personalities. Since I'm not very well-organized myself, such friends and I can complement and tremendously help each other. With me they do not feel shame, but feel free and loved for who they really are. They are wonderfully helpful to me with making plans and prioritizing. I, too, feel accepted.

"Sarah" was a young woman who was depressed because she couldn't seem to find a direction in life and constantly beat herself up about it. When she spoke about this she showed despair and self-disgust. She had a job she disliked and felt that she hadn't gotten anywhere, but she was unsure of what to do about it. She felt that she was not really good at anything, and this prevented her from having self-love or from having an active fantasy life; whenever she would begin to fantasize, she would make fun of herself in a cruel way. She felt so badly about herself that she was unable to look at her likes and dislikes or strengths and weaknesses, so she just avoided the whole thing.

At first she was unhappy that we had to talk about her childhood, instead of finding a way to somehow make her feel better without examining her life experiences. As time went on, she realized that her father seemed very hard to please. She realized that she had never had any aspirations of her own, and was blocked by wanting her father to be proud of her. Sarah frequently bore the brunt of her father's sense of humor, and he was unable to give her adequate credit for her achievements; to the extent that he did give credit, he seemed to be embarrassed by those feelings. Keep in mind that Sarah was a very bright young woman, but she thought poorly of herself. Her self-image was too linked to what her father happened to say, and she was stuck still wanting and trying to get validation the man was incapable of giving.

Sarah's father seemed well-intentioned, but didn't understand that Sarah's purpose in life was not to live up to his own fantasies that he had failed to realize. She felt that her father loved her, but was not proud of her. Sarah and I discussed pride for a long time, and how direction in life should not be chosen out of a desire to be proud of ourselves so much as what we like and feel we can do well, with a whole heart.

Sarah came to understand that her father also suffered from wanting something from his parents that they could not give, and that he was passing this on to her. With time, she realized that, no matter what she did, her father had his own choices and his own path, and that, if he didn't seek help for his issues, it was his business and not hers. She recognized that she could never fill the gap left by his own disappointment in his parents and in himself.

Recall Erikson's stages from Chapter 5. The issues we are talking about involve Sarah's sense of autonomy. You may be wondering why Sarah didn't simply choose a vocation her father wanted and be done with it? Actually, even though she had been stuck, the reason she did not do this was a good one. Part of Sarah did not want to please authority, and simply could not let herself do it. Unconsciously, she wanted very much to be her own person, and this side of her, split from the other side that craved her father's approval, kept warring within her.

To get unblocked, Sarah needed to become conscious of the different sides of her personality. If you are completely unconsciously driven, you live in conflict and without choices. When Sarah realized this, she experienced a great deal of relief, as she also realized that her father couldn't help how he was, and that she needed to focus on approving of herself now, as adults do. She was able to forgive her father and to go forward. Remember, if you feel stuck you most likely have a conflict between two different aspects of your personality – one representing your true desires and the other resentful of them.

Becoming conscious of her internal, underlying conflicts was extremely beneficial to Sarah, although it did not happen overnight. As a matter of fact, Sarah worked in the health field and had diagnosed herself with panic disorder, because every time she started to think about her lack of direction in life, she felt all hemmed in and trapped, and would then panic. When she had first called, she told me that she had been advised that the best treatment for panic disorder was cognitive behavioral therapy – learning to recognize her symptoms, control them, and realize they wouldn't last – combined with relaxation exercises and affirmations. Sarah asked some questions about the kind of therapy I do, and I told her that addressing the panic disorder was not enough, that we needed to know *why* she had panic attacks, and that I focused on insight.

Sarah initially decided to follow the cognitive-behavioral route instead. When she began the group therapy she had been advised to join, she immediately realized that she wanted to do well to have the approval of the therapist. She made an immediate connection to her father. She called me back, saying she now wanted to deal with the issues that caused her attacks.

As Sarah progressed, she not only forgave her father, but was able to tell him in a nice way what her career goals were. Her father was a successful businessman who really wanted her to follow in his footsteps, and she had decided instead that she wanted to teach disturbed children. She told him that she hoped for his blessing, but that she had discovered a true calling and was going to pursue it. Perhaps when her father realized he was freed from trying to make Sarah please *his* father by following in business, the pressure was off him. He gave her his blessing and showed interest in the education that Sarah began. It doesn't always go this way, and people still need to achieve autonomy and come to approve of themselves, but it is a wonderful bonus when it does happen.

Why do adults still crave, even strive for, a parent's approval and praise – especially when it is not forthcoming – and fail to move forward in their development as a result? One reason is that we never stop wanting what we didn't have as children. Then, thoughts and feelings – in this case, the need for parental regard – get repressed and denied and go into the unconscious. In Sarah's case, she didn't even know she had a conflict, just that she had been lacking in direction. When people like Sarah have an internal conflict, they don't know it consciously. She was afraid of not having her father's approval but also afraid to do something solely to win it. The power struggle, once with her father, was now within herself, and one she had to win. It is so important to know as much about yourself as you can, and Sarah presents to us an excellent example of the importance of self-knowledge.

This was not all of Sarah's work, but I do want to stress that we did not address career choice. Sarah's uncertainty about her path was related to unconscious conflict, so I did not try to help her find a career she liked, which wouldn't have been valuable in this context. Instead, her unconscious conflict was brought into her awareness and her ability to fantasize brought her into touch with her calling. One day she said she had been excited all week and that she "realized" (the unconscious made conscious) that she had always wanted to be a special education teacher. This just happened by itself after she began to heal the knotted-up and painful mass of feelings that prevented further growth. It is no wonder she felt panic – a panic so overwhelming it was impossible for her to think clearly.

Although she had her new life and was no longer in conflict, Sarah still had to grieve the fact that she had lived up until then trying to fulfill her father's dream instead of knowing herself. Her initial reaction was to judge herself, just as she used to, criticizing what she had been doing as "stupid." I explained to her that we are all "stupid" when we are ruled by unconscious feelings. She had to mourn what she saw as lost time, but I pointed out to her that the personal growth and awareness she achieved was quite an accomplishment indeed. Anyway, what good would earlier success in some field have done her without her hard-won insight? She saw that, just as her father had tried to do, you cannot mask painful underlying feelings with a shiny career. You can sure try, just as so very many people do, but it doesn't work.

It is very important to mourn or grieve what we didn't have but that we needed and wanted, or what we did have that was dysfunctional. Sarah worked through the earlier years when her father was so critical, when all she wanted was to be loved and to see in his behavior that she was all right as she was. Though she didn't go through this process with her father, as she had forgiven him and didn't wish to hurt him, Sarah's father also benefited from her therapy. He was delighted that she was emotionally free, and one day confided to her that he didn't really want to go into business either, and wanted to please his own father. Her father grew in insight and was thrilled with Sarah's progress. While she never criticized him and realized she had her own issues, he did come to apologize. As I said, this does not always happen, and was a very happy bonus for Sarah, but she would have gotten better anyway without it.

While this struggle is all about the ability to fantasize and to have fuller access to one's own mind, it is also about self-esteem, or what I prefer to call self-love or self-respect. It is not about someone else telling you he approves of your choice, and it is not about being proud. It is really about having a certainty about who you are, what you like, and what is meaningful to you. It is about recovering your own wonderful self and knowing yourself.

As you might imagine, Sarah did not have an easy time in therapy. She would ask me when she would be "all better" and if I couldn't just "take away" all the anxiety. I wished that I could, but told her that it would deprive her of her own process. Her anxiety was trying to help her live as a full, authentic, and autonomous person. Taking away her process, even if I could, wouldn't help her.

In the course of therapy Sarah's insight grew and grew, and it became apparent that Sarah was very gifted psychologically. Realizing that issues begin in childhood, she wondered how many children in special education couldn't focus because of issues that troubled them, not just because of a "chemical imbalance." This realization hit her very hard, and she decided to work with younger children with special needs. She is now doing so very successfully and with great joy.

Does Sarah worry about self-esteem now? Not at all. Her therapy was difficult and sometimes painful, but she knows she displayed extraordinary honesty and courage in reaching for her higher self, and she heard the inner voice of a calling. She teaches special education because it is the right thing for her to be doing. As Sarah learned, this path is much more important than doing something for pride. She knows she is aware, brave, and has vulnerabilities. She uses humor to address things she doesn't like in herself. She also knows she sometimes feels impatient with new teachers, but controls it. She does the best she can, and when children learn she is joyous for them and sees it as their victory, with herself as facilitator. She feels sadness, not self-blame, when children don't progress.

In our culture, so many people are hooked on self-esteem, which so often means doing something better than everyone else. This makes it very difficult to admire and enjoy someone, and hard to feel gratitude. It makes it almost impossible to experience the joy of complementarity without envy and sad comparisons, and it makes people seek validation from anyone and everyone. When you reach inside for answers, find them, and do the work to progress emotionally, you achieve self-love, though then it can be sad when you see others living a defensive life.

"Dan" also came to me with a self-diagnosed anxiety disorder, and knew he wanted to work on issues. He intensely wanted to be in a serious relationship with someone, and was a kind and intelligent man with many attractive features. However, he would go on a date with a woman and start assessing whether or not she liked him. He would do this whether or not he liked her or had anything in common with her. He craved validation so badly, wanting someone to want him, that there was nothing else in his world, certainly not mature love. He did not see how he sometimes led people on, only to have to tell them later he wanted to break off the relationship. He himself was very angry when someone did this to him, only later realizing that this was what *he* himself had been doing. After this, when another woman he had been dating broke off the relationship, he came to understand that she was not trying to hurt him, but simply couldn't let his or anyone else's feelings matter too much because she also lived for validation.

Dan took a hard look at his life. He had been raised by confused and anxious parents and never felt secure in their love, which seemed to have very many conditions. Underlyingly, he was terribly depressed, and he came to face this. He, like many others, lacked awareness of his underlying feelings, and unconsciously thought he could find a woman to make him feel better. He didn't realize that he was in no position to care for anyone, because he didn't even know himself and only wanted someone to silence the terrible feelings he lived with all the time. There was no room for someone else's issues.

Ironically, as Dan gave up seeking validation and faced his real feelings, remembering the times those feelings had been hurt, he experienced humility and gratitude. He told me of a friend who had "put up" with him for years, and he thanked this friend for doing so. He found in himself a very caring, sensitive individual, and said that he didn't used to be "very nice."

Dan really came into his own. He has had a few relationships in which he and a woman were able to share and to be good to each other. While even this was a new joy for him, he has not yet met someone to be with forever. He knows that he is able to love, sees himself as rather shy, and feels that he has a chance to connect with another. In any case, his other relationships are improved. He also had to grieve when he realized what he had missed in the name of self-esteem. He came to have self-love and felt so good about what he had accomplished and how he had changed, that he became very patient with those in his family who had not changed. He liked himself because of real things, not illusions.

Perhaps now you can see how self-acceptance and the ability to have fantasies interact. I hope you have seen that if you are someone who has painful and unconscious feelings of self-dislike, good feelings won't follow. You can distract yourself all you want, but the anxiety won't go away until you listen to what is causing it. When you can fully live and experience life and know yourself as well as possible, the fantasy life which is your birthright comes easily. Your fantasies can be fun, silly, or motivational – they can be about anything at all. Your feelings are integrated and you have self-love and self-acceptance, which are found within you. In the early years, it is possible to have parents who give you these things as a gift – a very great one – but if you did not, you must achieve them yourself. As many others have done, you, too, can certainly do it.

Exercises

Exercise 1

Imagine that for some reason you have lost that which most boosts how you wish to see yourself and have others see you – your athletic ability, your health, your home, your expensive car. What are your thoughts and feelings now? Who are you and what is the essence of you that is exactly the same? That is the real you.

Exercise 2

Think of a time when you tried to get someone to like you. This does not have to be a romantic interest, but any kind of relationship. Did you like the person? Think of a time when you *did* get someone to like you who you later realized you did not like. What did you do? Was this ever done to you? If so, did you realize that perhaps the person was doing what you yourself have done? What can happen when you try to get validation from someone you may not even like?

Exercise 3

Think of a fantasy, develop it, and write it. Is it happy, silly, inspirational?

Exercise 4

Think of five activities or jobs. Say why you would or wouldn't like each one.

Exercise 5

How do you wish you could spend each day? What prevents you from having that kind of day? Could you incorporate aspects of the fantasy into your real life?

Chapter 9

Relationships & Being Needed

Unlike earlier chapters, which have focused on individual spokes of the PCS wheel, this one discusses how these spokes or issues become problematic in our relationships with significant others. Relationship problems and needing to feel needed are typical of the PCS person, who will often try to force the partner into a role that supports their defensive system, with little or no awareness as to how this impacts the other person.

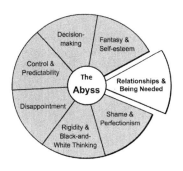

Frequently couples enter therapy announcing that they have, for example, a "communication" problem. However, it is my experience that one or both parties usually have strong and persistent individual issues – often the spokes of the PCS wheel – that become exacerbated because they can and often do prevent a healthy relationship. How can someone be in a relationship if he spends life avoiding his real, core Self?

I am always amazed and saddened to see how people constantly try to get their partner to meet their needs – to follow their "script" – with no awareness at all as to what the other person's needs might be. By the time couples come to me, they are often both so angry that they don't even *want* to meet the other's needs, and the way they would like to think of themselves has been trampled and ruined. Rarely do couples really empathize with how the other feels, but want only to be made to feel a certain way. I have known people so hungry for validation that they cannot even determine how they feel about someone else. Their need is simply too strong and overpowering to really be able to empathize with another person.

People marry with no thought or training about their own needs, but then become angry and upset when the partner does not – perhaps *can*not – gratify them. It is not surprising that a great number of relationships are troubled. All the issues that people have find their way into relationships and can cause trouble there. It is important to understand your own dynamics for many reasons, but certainly so that you can be aware of them and make conscious and thoughtful choices about how to behave.

As stated earlier, many PCS people need validation to shore up a fragile self-image. This issue is very important here, too, as this need also affects the partner. If you are in a relationship and your aim is only to keep feeding a shaky self-image, what do you bring to the relationship? Maybe you do many nice things and try to be perfect so that your partner will validate you. Maybe your partner has to swallow her own needs to constantly validate yours.

I have had countless clients tell me that someone broke off a relationship with them after they had been careful to always do nice things for them. When asked why they had gone overboard, they would say something like, "So he'd think I'm good and want to stay with me." Or, "To feel good about myself." Or even, "Because I like to be needed." I always ask, "And did the other person get a chance to be needed?" Or, "How did the other person get to feel good about *herself*?"

These clients were always surprised by my question. They thought they were being nice just because they were doing *things* for another, never stopping to wonder whether the other person's emotional needs were being met, as their own were too strong to allow that perspective. An intense need for validation erases the personality of the other, who quickly learns to express no needs or preferences at all, and can only keep offering praise and gratitude, which turns to emptiness and rage over time.

You cannot just be validated, needed, or appreciated in a relationship; you also need to validate, to need, and to appreciate the other. If all of your interactions are aimed at making you feel good about yourself, or what you receive emotionally, what emotional needs of the other are being met? How does this affect the other person? While you are interacting to build your own sense of worth, the other person may be feeling incompetent, unloved, and not needed or appreciated.

I am not suggesting that you have ever deliberately hurt or used people. I think that if you have hurt others, it was because the emotional pain you were in blinded you to their feelings and needs. However, when you have greater self-awareness, you truly have more choices as to how you interact with others. And, the truth is, people with a need to be validated all the time are not really loving someone else, but merely fueling themselves and their needs. These needs can destroy parts of yourself, such as your ability to really love, as well as the self-respect of the other.

Recall the client who would begin dating a woman and at the very beginning his only thought was that he wanted her to like him, whether he liked her or not. He was so set on this that he didn't stop to evaluate whether or not she was right for him. Did he intend to lead someone on whom he didn't want to continue with? No, of course not. In fact, outside of this situation, he was extraordinarily kind and caring. Still, it took someone doing that to *him* for him to see what he had been doing to others. It showed him what it felt like to be on the receiving end of such behavior, and helped him to see that his behavior had little to do with the other person, but related back to the way he felt about himself. If your emotional needs are so strong that you cannot see the feelings of others, or who they really are as whole people with patterns of their own, it is time for more self-awareness.

Always remember that everyone else has issues and feelings, too. When you go on a date and try to make the other person care for you, they are likely to believe you are extremely interested. Really, the other person should only begin to get that impression when you *are* very interested and would like to continue seeing one another. The more self-aware you are, the more power and presence you have in your relationships.

"Tom" is a successful professional and calls himself a "rescuer." He forms relationships with women who are extremely disturbed, as his mother was. He could never fix his mother, but unconsciously feels that if he keeps trying to help very disturbed women, he will somehow have atoned for his inability to change his mother. Time and time again, Tom would become involved with a woman who used drugs, was unable to hold a job, and who periodically became enraged and out of control. But these women would also at times become needy and depressed, which was the part he liked. He would try to be rational and understanding, yet would keep being mistreated. He would ask why she behaved like this, and I would ask *him* why he was with her and had been with so many others like her. Luckily, Tom came to me alone, because his partner refused to come.

Tom had experienced deep shame during his upbringing by a chaotic mother and various men. He was made to feel in charge at a young age, handling household affairs for his mother, but then was the object of her wrath and humiliation. He was mistreated by the mother's boyfriends as well. He survived a hellish childhood by developing a PCS personality. He became highly and rigidly organized in his practical affairs and in his views. When he grew up and dated more normal women, they rejected him because of his rigidity, for being what they called a "control freak." This fed right into Tom's deep sense of shame, as his perfectionism made him feel inept and unworthy, unable to relate to a healthier woman.

While none of this was conscious on his part, Tom made a very important decision: He would find a woman who was in so much trouble emotionally that she would never leave him, because her neediness would prevent her from wanting to be on her own. If he could be so needed for someone's very survival, he would be validated, or so he thought, and his own emotional issues would shrink by comparison. He had trouble making decisions, but this woman would ignore his advice when she demanded he give it and do what she wished, so all of these poor decisions could be attributed to her.

Tom had managed to recreate his sad childhood. Just as he would make dinner for his mother and himself when he was a young child, taking over her job, so that she would always come back to him, he continued in a miserable relationship because he was sure all the needs he met would keep this woman from leaving.

It has become part of the psychological jargon to call people "rescuers." Though I have no objection to the word, it does not adequately express the deeply-rooted and painful dynamics that need to be addressed for this behavior to change. As I have said before, children feel they deserve what they get. Their feelings about themselves are formed by how they were treated. Without addressing his issues, Tom had little chance of letting himself feel he deserved to be in a relationship with anyone better than his abusive but needy mother. The rigidity and control he tried to exert in these relationships were sometimes experienced as needed structure by these women, but only a disturbed adult will want that kind of rigidity, and there is a huge price to pay.

Initially, Tom wanted me to tell him how to behave so that his partner would behave better. It took a while, but he came to see that he could not control her issues, that he could only control his own. He came to face the despair and insecurity that he had been hiding from all his life. He faced his personal Abyss, of feeling like an unwanted and unworthy child who was mistreated and of being thrown into absolute chaos. As time went on, Tom did become less rigid and controlling, and he became more aware of the feelings of others, which always tends to happen in the course of therapy. He did not want to control anyone and wanted to do better himself.

He eventually left this relationship and continued to work on himself. When he began to date again, he was surprised to see how he often would end up with someone very troubled, but he would not let those relationships develop. He finally met someone with better mental health – a PCS person who had been a rescuer herself, had had therapy, and now wanted something better. There were challenges for them, but they would often use humor and joke about trading off who got to make which decision, and they are very empathic toward each other.

Tom is but one example of how having PCS dynamics can lead a highly-functioning person into a disastrous relationship. Avoiding issues and hiding from yourself, then making a choice out of extreme loneliness, often leads to a very unhealthy and painful situation. I am glad to say that, as a result of his hard work, Tom reclaimed his knowledge of his dignity and self-worth. He redefined himself as a person who was not perfect, but who cared and was willing to work on his issues. He and his new partner let each other feel needed and have achieved a healthy inter-dependence rather than a co-dependent relationship. Because Tom had the courage to address his real issues and feelings about himself, he no longer needed to select partners who were disturbed; he chose to give and receive mature love instead of trying to obtain validation at any price.

In treating couples, it is always important to consider individual issues, which is why I prefer to work with individuals. I have seen countless couples in which one party complains about the extreme dysfunction of the other – drug or alcohol abuse, compulsive cheating, lying about finances and spending, mental abuse, and even run-ins with the law. They desperately want the partner to change – or think they do. But, how much change could they tolerate? It is all too common for the supposedly dysfunctional partner to really change, and then the PCS person, the healthier one, begins to feel unhappy and insecure, fearing that the improved partner will no longer want or need him or her. Settling for someone whose problems make you feel better about your own is a poor substitute for love.

"Craig," divorced for two years and a former "rescuer," is dating some-one he loves being with. He feels joy, empathy, and respect, and de-lights in her intelligence; he loves when she is happy. He said, "I never had this before," to which I replied, "You never wanted it before." "I never valued it before, and I feel so alive," he concluded. Craig now has awareness of what it is like to be truly present with another person.

Another serious relationship issue relates to what people refer to as a martyr complex. "Jean" was raised in a poor neighborhood by a very strong and hardworking mother. Her father died when she was ten. Her mother was strict, as she wanted to protect her children against negative influences; because the mother worked two jobs, the children had many responsibilities and worked hard as well. This tired and well-intentioned mother had little time or energy for feelings, to praise her children, or to be openly affectionate. She gave all of her life and strength to them. Jean developed a PCS personality, one very similar to her mother's. She was an outstanding student and went to college on scholarship, then helped her two younger siblings attend college too. Yet, she had never learned to think about herself or others outside of a helping role. She was a wonderful person with little personal insight.

Jean's mother wished for her daughter to have a relationship with a man and to be happy, and when Jean first met Dan, it seemed like a happy event. However, Dan's plan to attend school part-time fell through, as did the many different jobs he held. Jean believed that he would settle down and work, but it just didn't happen, and Dan would only make excuses. Time passed. They now had two children, and Jean was the only one working. Dan had begun to drink and to be verbally abusive to her. He took out his poor self-regard from not contributing to the family on Jean. Jean's mother took care of the children while Jean worked, and Jean would then care for the family at night.

Unlike some of the cases we have considered, Jean did have a very good mother. Yet, as a child, Jean would look at how hard her mother worked and feel guilty and ashamed for wanting to play instead of helping in the house or doing homework, etc. She felt that her mother was such an excellent person that she herself was unworthy. Jean's perfectionism was of course rewarded by teachers and other adults and it got her far, but her feeling of unworthiness remained with her.

Jean really saw herself as lazy, unworthy, and unkind, even though she was none of these things. In her mind, she likened her patience with Dan to her mother's patience in raising her, an unfair analogy. She felt she deserved nothing better. To assuage her underlying feelings, she did volunteer work in addition to working and caring for her family, though she had no time or strength to do this. There was little or no pleasure in her life, which unconsciously is what she wanted, because her mother had little pleasure and Jean felt so undeserving of any. Friends and neighbors kept telling her to leave her husband, and she wondered why she had so much difficulty in doing so.

Because Jean did have a good mother who was very concerned about her daughter, we invited the mother into Jean's therapy. The mother told her how she had been the best child anyone could have asked for, how sweet and helpful she had been, and how she never knew what she had ever done to have a child so wonderful. This was extremely powerful. I saw both women in therapy, and they both reached the point where they could let themselves deserve each other. Jean at long last got the emotional relationship with her mother she had so badly wanted, and the mother got to receive genuine gratitude from a daughter who loved her very much.

Jean did finally leave her husband, and she and her mother together embarked on an emotional journey in which both were happy and deserving. The mother helped Jean with her children, but Jean also took her children to an excellent daycare center, so that both had time to enjoy the children, each other, and life in general. Jean, her mother, and her children blossomed. Jean did eventually meet a nice man, but was in no hurry to be in a relationship, and at the time we terminated therapy she was taking things slowly. I later received a call from her, saying that she is done with the "martyr stuff," and she told me how wonderfully her mother, herself, and the children were doing.

Jean had formed a terrible image of herself in her mind because her mother was so hardworking. Her Abyss – being a "lazy, unappreciative" person – was avoided by caring for a troubled man who would not do his share. She not only saved herself by her new awareness, but saved her mother and children as well.

When I think of "rescuers" and needing to be needed, a gay couple I saw in therapy comes to mind – "Mike" and "Tony." Mike had taken care of a very disturbed mother, and for many years lived a "straight" lifestyle and had relationships with women. Unfortunately, he chose women much like his mother who were very disturbed; he was also coming to accept that he was gay and was dealing with this realization. When he "came out" he thought it was a good time to stop rescuing people and to have a normal and healthy relationship. He met Tony, a very nice, high-functioning individual, but things were not to prove so easy. Tony had had a series of relationships with men who had serious problems in living – in keeping a job, an apartment, even friends. He would support them and stay in relationships where he got nothing and gave all. He had also decided he was ready to have a relationship with a normal and responsible person.

When Mike and Tony first met, it seemed like they had both found their dream, but it was not as easy as they thought it might be. In their first session they each told me how the other did not appreciate him, how each felt he was not needed, unappreciated, and unnecessary in the other's life. They both needed to be needed, but neither one had learned to need. They also thought that being needed meant that the other person wouldn't be able to function alone, a false and dangerous belief.

In the course of therapy, we brought to light all of the PCS dynamics both had, and why. They saw that they could either continue pursuing a sense of self-worth by being with very disturbed people, or they could each learn to need and appreciate and become more balanced. With effort and sometimes with humor, both of them met the challenge, came to easily understand the feelings of the other – they were, after all, so much alike – and their relationship improved greatly. It is not enough to want something better than what we have been doing; often it is necessary to understand the *why* of our behavior to really affect a change.

Another relationship issue that often comes up is letting others discuss negative feelings with you. Some PCS people feel guilty even having a thought or feeling they think is negative. This runs counter to a healthy psychology, because acknowledging your thoughts and feelings to yourself is a necessity if you don't want your unconscious going against you; it does not mean you will act on those feelings. You have more control when you acknowledge the way you feel than when you run from these feelings or cover them up in some way.

Have you ever been in a relationship and tried to make someone feel guilty for something that really was in a gray area, not something really terrible? What we call reaction formation is when a person has a strong feeling about something, feels guilty as a result, and then takes the opposite point of view.

When I was in graduate school, a small group of us were standing around talking and joking between classes, near finals time. We were saying how one more assignment would kill us, etc. Then another student joined us. She stated that she *loved* homework and got excited about each assignment, basically taking away the venting session we had all been enjoying. Needless to say, this got on everyone's nerves, and someone said to her that we were just letting off steam.

We have all known people like this, who never acknowledge one single negative thought. You really can't get very close to them because they won't be real with you. They are not trying to be mean or superior, but are so afraid of their own negative thoughts and feelings that they cannot tolerate those of others. These negative thoughts and feelings are a part of life. The world is far from perfect, and if people perceive you as unsupportive of their true feelings they will stop sharing them with you.

Have you ever denied the feelings of people you are close to? If so, what was the result? Remember, a range of human emotion is the normal and healthy experience. Believe it or not, kind, moral people have angry, frustrated, disappointed, and hateful feelings from time to time. They may not act on them, but all of us share in these normal human emotions. There is no such thing as a person who is so "nice" that every single one of their thoughts and feelings are also "nice."

When you begin to understand that behavior is separate from feelings, and that behavior represents a decision and a choice, you can begin to give yourself permission for some of the negative feelings you have. You can always behave in a morally-upstanding way if it is your choice to do so, but can still acknowledge to yourself that you don't always feel as "nice" as you behave when you are with others.

Now let's look at another defense mechanism that can interfere with relationships – projection. We discussed projection briefly in the chapter on dynamics, and will now look at it in greater depth. We use projection when we don't like something about ourselves, and then attribute it to others. For example, if we don't care for someone and can't admit this to ourselves, we may then say that the person dislikes us. No, it's not always convenient or pleasurable to acknowledge you dislike someone; if it is your boss, or your dear friend's significant other, you of course would prefer to like that person. But if you do not, it is important to admit this to yourself. You can continue to behave in a decent way when you are with this person, because we all deserve respect. But we also deserve to be permitted to have our own personal preferences, and we can't like every single person.

If you hear something bad about a person, are you quick to condemn them to feel better about yourself? Have you ever openly judged someone for their feelings when they needed you to understand them? When people feel badly about themselves, they often behave this way to take the hurt off themselves. This, of course, is very wrong, and will do nothing for you but lower the way you think of yourself already. A lot of damage has been done this way, and people who are aware wouldn't do these things. What if you behaved this way to a PCS perfectionist? What if these dynamics are occurring between two married people? You can see the potential for destructiveness to a relationship.

Do you believe that you are supposed to go through life liking everyone, or liking everyone equally? If this is the case, you could be repressing, denying, and splitting off your negative feelings. But the mind demands honesty from us, maybe not to share with others, but certainly with ourselves. Have you ever been accused of being passive-aggressive? People like this don't really mean any harm, but they have resentful feelings that they bottle up and deny. Then one day...*bam!* – a hostile little backstab slips out. When people are the target of a passive-aggressive attack, it seems to come out of nowhere. Whatever their transgression, it was probably a long time before, and the target of the attack thinks that the relationship has been good.

This is one reason it is very important to be honest with yourself. If you are not, the real feeling, even if it wasn't conscious, can come rushing out. When this happens, you can do things that not only annoy people, but alienate them; most important, you lose control of your behavior. If you admit to yourself how you feel, your self-control is under your *conscious* control, and this is very important.

If you engage in passive-aggressive behavior – even though it originates in your intense criticism of yourself – people will feel betrayed. While you cannot rightfully blame anyone for their feelings, we all have choices in how we behave. If you are in touch with your genuine feelings, you then can know the pleasure of having behaved rightfully or taken the high road in spite of more primitive feelings pulling you in another direction. This builds self-esteem. Being in touch with your real feelings and acting in a decent way leads to true self-love and self-respect.

One more defense you need to know about is projective identification, which we also touched on in Chapter 5. Recall that projection involves verbally judging someone for a so-called negative feeling to get the blame off yourself temporarily. Projective identification goes further than projection, and will have a more negative effect on you and your relationships. Projective identification is a defense in which you actually provoke someone to do something that you can then blame them for, so that it fits in with how you want to think of yourself.

When I was in college, an acquaintance of mine would tell us when someone had bullied her emotionally. She would recite a litany of offenses, and we would sympathize with her, saying, "Oh, that was so mean! So-and-So has no regard at all for others." After we empathized with her and took her side, this young woman would look at us disapprovingly and say, "You're horrible! How can you say those things?" This is projective identification – making someone else take your feelings and then blaming them. This woman made us feel *her* anger so she could be free of it.

I did not know what projective identification was back then, but I did know that this behavior was unacceptable in a friend, and I didn't really want to carry around this idea of being horrible. I spoke to her about the incident, telling her that if she wanted to tell a story and evoke sympathy, even outrage, from her friends, she should stop calling us "horrible" when we jump to her defense.

It is important to own your feelings. It is your choice whether or not you share them, but you must own them and be aware of them if you want to have choices about how you interact in this world. You may have done things like the woman above to a lesser extent, and that is harmless. As long as you are aware of what you're doing, and the person in the interaction is all right with it, it is not destructive.

For example, someone who wishes to procrastinate over a project with her partner might jokingly say to the other, "Don't you feel like going to the movies?" The other person might laughingly say, "You're terrible!" as she reaches for her purse to head to the theater. We have all heard people jokingly say, "I really had to twist your arm to get you to do that," and both will laugh.

When this kind of interaction is conscious, notice the difference. In the earlier example, someone felt used and manipulated. Here, both are in touch with their feelings, and act of their own free will. They therefore see the humor in their interaction. You could say to a friend that you feel like going out and spending money, when you are both trying to save, and the other person could say, "I do, too. Let's go for a small treat." Or the other person could say, "No, I feel like it, too, but let's wait and stick to our budgets and get a reward later." Again, this is a conscious and honest interaction; therefore, it does no harm. Can you imagine how this interaction could be changed into a damaging one with real projective identification?

When you take responsibility for your own actions, you do not blame anyone else for them – and, let's face it, no one likes to be blamed. When you take responsibility, even if someone does blame you, all you have to do is say, "Yes, I know I did that, and, like I said, I'm sorry." Try it sometime. When you deny your feelings and don't take responsibility, those whom your actions affect are left unsatisfied, the blaming continues, and relationships are damaged. If you own your actions and thoughts, the blaming will just fizzle out.

Has this kind of behavior interfered with *your* relationships? I suggest you think about this and take a few notes. Remember, this is not about judging yourself, but about deciding that you now want to be in touch with your feelings for your own personal growth, for the sake of better relationships, and to begin to really love yourself. Remember, a martyr, victim, or rescuer often provokes the other into behavior that follows this script.

If you have the tendencies described in this book, being wrong is very painful to you. I know this is hard, but I can only tell you that never being wrong infuriates other people. No one wants to be wrong all the time, and so very many people have the same issue you do. Since we all make many mistakes, if you force others to take the blame and you never do, two things will certainly happen: people will lose respect for you, and they will be angry and distance themselves from you.

One young man told me tearfully how his mother taught him never to back down, that no one will love you if you do. This is obviously a false belief, but it was so strong that, when he took the plunge and apologized for something he had done to his wife, he was shocked that it actually brought them closer and she loved him even more.

Some people are afraid of being wrong because they think it means they are terrible people – which brings them once again to their fear of the Abyss. This is why insight is so important. People behave this way only because of intense emotional pain. While I sympathize with this pain, it is still wrong to let it guide your interactions in such a way that it harms the other person. It will have a destructive effect on others, and ultimately on you. The problem is that it doesn't take the feelings of others into account. Just as someone once may have hurt you by making you feel you were always wrong or bad, you are now continuing the pattern and doing damage to others. I cannot stress enough that your self-love will increase tremendously when you take responsibility for your feelings and behavior.

"Leslie" had a dread and hatred of being wrong. She had gotten to the point that she could admit this to herself and could tell me with ease, but admitting it to her husband was quite another matter. It was as if she knew she was about to leave her black-and-white thinking behind forever and move on, which is a wonderful step, but still scary and still a loss. I have asked her to take a huge leap of faith into what for her is the unknown, and she is doing it. When I asked if she was ready for this leap, Leslie replied with a drawn-out "Y-e-s-s," and I knew she would move forward as she always does. Her excellent ethical sense gives her strength – and *you* have that same strength. The healthy part of her strong conscience made her realize that she and her loved ones deserved better, and she took the plunge. She once told me of a time when she had made fun of her husband so that she wouldn't blame herself, and how horrible she had felt. She realized then that she had reached the point where she could do better and recognized that her self-esteem would improve.

Leslie told me sadly how she can now see others more clearly and realizes that everyone has hang-ups, some of them serious. She said that when she used to be anxious she thought it was just her. She tearfully explained how she has lived her whole life trying to feel she is as good as others, and all along there were people hurting a great deal more than she was, and people who are just like she was who are not doing anything about it. I told her that perhaps they weren't ready or lacked the courage, and she accepted this with wisdom and maturity, though it weighed on her. She saw that the way out of anxiety is truth, and that that which is repressed is never something happy.

Now that she has discovered the joy and power in self-awareness, and has emotionally passed the achievements of so many, she no longer desires to be better than anyone else. She does wish she had more people in her life who do not have so many defensive areas that must be avoided. The bubble of black-and-white thinking has burst, and she is now dealing with her disappointment. She has had many disappointments, many of them devastating, but is confronting them with her usual honesty and courage. When you face your disappointment and sadness, what you are left with is just that: disappointment and sadness – but not the anxiety and fear of the Abyss. You no longer fear breaking the fragile defense that you have to be perfect and that everyone else must be perfect, too.

I saw from the first day the real self of this wonderful young woman, and I await the happy day when she will see an accurate reflection of herself in the mirror. She thinks it was funny, though sad, that she spent so many years thinking she was so bad, so inferior. As the person holding up the mirror, I could only tell her that I knew giving up the fantasy of perfection by participating in real life was sad, but had incredible and happy rewards. She has only a glimpse now of her own inner beauty, but she will soon see herself for who she truly is.

I discussed the issue of control earlier in this book, but it is important to dwell a bit now on this issue, as it affects the relationships of the PCS person. Many PCS people wish to control, not out of malice, but out of insecurity. Nevertheless, no one likes to be controlled, and a self-respecting person will eventually leave such a relationship behind. Ironically, the attempt to control others is meant to keep them from leaving, yet it is often the thing that drives them away. Control issues can present problems with friends, a partner, or children – anyone with whom we have a relationship.

As we have seen, wanting a large degree of control over others has its roots in a time when one felt little or no control. Yet, we can only control ourselves. While I have seen this knowledge cause sadness in many, it is the truth, and is therefore worth accepting. A very painful fact of life is that we have all felt helpless at some point. Many people remember adults in their lives abusing the control they held over them as children, and live with a determination that this will never happen again. Yet, we are helpless to change or force others, and ultimately we must all accept this. I have seen people stay in highly dysfunctional relationships – not for love, but because they simply couldn't accept that they couldn't control the other person. Furthermore, trying to control others unreasonably is a violation of their rights.

While perhaps none of us deals with helplessness very well, it is crucial in life to know when you truly can't do anything and learn to just let go. I remember being a young adult when my mother died of cancer. Before her death, I kept frantically thinking of something I could do so she could live and be well. I had always seen her as being able to help me and keep me safe, and one day I said to my husband, "If this were me dying, my mother wouldn't just be sitting around grieving and trying to accept it and doing nothing!" My husband wisely said to me, "But in the reverse situation, what could your mother do?" I needed that reminder to accept my helplessness and the inevitability of her impending death, but I had control over whether to be a comfort to her and over how I handled myself.

Sometimes people try to control too much, feeling that if they love hard enough, they can solve all the problems of their loved ones. It is a hard and painful lesson, but people are on the level where they need to be. If someone asks for help or advice, you can give it, but taking away someone's emotional process, even if it worked, would not help them gain anything.

Throughout this book, you have seen examples of how the various spokes of the wheel are connected with one another, and how they all represent aspects of the same central issue. When you are in a relationship with another human being, particularly a romantic relationship, in which so many hopes, dreams, and expectations all revolve around the other person, these issues are compounded and can become more extreme.

If two people with PCS dynamics become involved romantically, we now have two sets of interrelated PCS dynamics interfering in their ability to connect in an honest way. This is very sad indeed, especially when it is apparent that underneath it all, these two people truly do care about one another. However, as these dynamics do interfere with authentic interaction, they can be poisonous in an intimate relationship.

We often hear the troubled state of relationships discussed in the media – statistics on the divorce rate, for example. It is true that people seem to be experiencing a great deal of difficulty in remaining together. Perhaps you are learning how it is that adults have so much trouble staying together. It is not so difficult to see how it is that they come together to begin with – not when we have so many people invested in the idea of the perfect partner, the perfect relationship, the perfect life. But what happens when the "honeymoon is over," and you are each becoming increasingly aware of the other's faults and your incompatibilities?

Most of our faults are innocuous, and are not "deal breakers." But when you have expected and desired perfection and are left with a mere human being – a person who, like yourself, has many areas of weakness, in addition to all the areas of strength – the resulting disappointment can cause tremendous feelings of indignation, unfairness, even a sense of having been wronged or cheated.

No one has tried to cheat you, but when the other person has brought his issues to the table, it can indeed seem like an affront to the person with PCS dynamics. It is also true that you fear your partner seeing *your* faults. So how do you work through these disappointments?

Again, these issues have been addressed in previous chapters. But it is one thing to work through your *own* sense of shame, of the perfectionistic, black-and-white thinking that has gotten you into trouble in the past; to look at your own hopes and fears, and fantasy life – to get closer to your own fear of the Abyss. It is another entirely to carry these new areas of progress forward into your relationship with the other, who may or may not have done work on himself.

Clients often come in for individual therapy due to the difficulties they are having in their current relationship. It is often the case that the troubled relationship they wish to work on is not really the problem at all, but merely points to areas of needed personal growth. The key to this is to look at patterns. If you can see that there are common patterns to your past relationships, you may want to take a look at what has caused you to repeat these behaviors, and what prevents you from entering authentically into a relationship with another person.

"Eileen" came to her first session talking about her boyfriend, "Jonathan." She felt hurt that Jonathan did not seem to understand her, nor did he ever take the time to try to talk with her about what was on her mind. She felt that she was always chasing after him, that he made himself unavailable to her, and grew aloof whenever she tried to get closer. Whenever he distanced himself emotionally, she pushed for even greater intimacy, and spent their time together sharing with him her hopes for the future and telling him how much she loved him. The more she did this, the more he withdrew. She asked me what was wrong with her that made Jonathan move away?

I asked Eileen to tell me about some of her past relationships. Had she had similar problems with men in the past? Eileen nodded emphatically. "Men are all the same," she said. "At the beginning when we first fall in love, it's so exciting, we're together all the time, and we share everything, all our thoughts and feelings. Then after a while they act like I'm doing something wrong just by trying to be close to them. The more I push for commitment the more they back away." She said she was tired of men and the games that they play. She saw this as an issue that had to do with men in general – that men feared commitment and intimacy.

I then asked Eileen to think about the areas of commonality in these different relationships. She had said that at the beginning, when they were first dating, she enjoyed getting close to these men. I said that it sounded like this intensity happened very quickly, before they had really had a chance to get to know one another. This made Eileen uncomfortable. While she agreed with what I had said, it was clearly an area of some concern to her. She looked embarrassed and said, "Well, now that you put it that way, it's true, I guess we have sort of rushed things at the beginning."

I see this so often in relationships, and it is very sad. Rather than getting to know one another gradually, over time, there is a tendency to rush into things and force a false intimacy before it is natural to feel intimate with one another. Eileen had said that she and Jonathan had fallen in love very quickly, but this is not what love is all about. Love is something that happens with time, with honesty and respect and an ability to accept a person with all her faults and weaknesses. You do not meet a person and fall in love right away, and when you tell one another that this is how you feel, naturally things are going to fall apart as the relationship continues.

Eileen came to see that as the other person withdrew from a situation he was beginning to feel less and less positive about, she pushed even harder for him to re-create with her the closeness and excitement they had had at the beginning. But people cannot maintain this false high forever. The more time you spend with another person, the more you get to see them for who they really are. And it's very likely, when you have rushed into things, that you have ascribed to them many of the qualities you would *like* for them to have, whether they were true or not. As you get to know them better, and come to find that they actually lack those qualities, you may try to force things. But this person cannot become the person you had hoped he might be. That is why the best course is to let relationships develop gradually, so that you can see for yourself, as you learn more about one another, whether you make a good fit.

After several months in therapy, Eileen ended things with Jonathan. She said she was very hurt by his reaction – he was relieved. Eileen had chosen someone who was emotionally unavailable, who, like herself, enjoyed intensity and false intimacy, but who wasn't ready to be real with another person. Rather than face this with honesty, he engaged in this game with Eileen, one in which he let her chase after him, and then removed himself emotionally more and more from the relating. Eileen, for her part, missed the high of the early stages of the relationship, and tried to control Jonathan's changing feelings by showing him how much she cared about him and how wonderful she could be.

Neither Eileen nor Jonathan had entered into the relationship with their real selves. They had brought their unrealistic expectations with them into the relationship, and some outworn, tired ideas about what a relationship could or should be. They treated the relationship as a game, and as a result, got little more out of it than one would expect from a game of any kind. Games are not real life, and so you do not get a real relationship when you treat it like a game. Mutual respect was lacking, as was the ability to appreciate one another as complete human beings, for both the good and the bad.

Eileen grew to see that this relationship with Jonathan was not about him, nor were her previous relationships that had followed the same pattern about her partners. She saw that it was her own desire to feel intimate with another person that drew her to these types of men, with whom she could instantly develop a very intense relationship. Unfortunately, beyond that early, exciting stage, these men were not capable of a deeper level of interaction. Eileen saw that to truly experience intimacy with another person, she had to learn to be patient, and to let things unfold naturally. She said quite wisely, "It feels better to be alone and to enjoy things I like to do, than to be with someone else and be trying to force them to like me." She saw that she had sought validation from these men, when it was up to her to feel more positively about herself.

After Eileen broke up with Jonathan, the focus of her therapy shifted from men and relationships to herself and her own thoughts and feelings – and her childhood. Eileen's parents had divorced when she was very young, and had set up an irregular custody arrangement. Though Eileen was meant to visit her father every other weekend, she often saw him only once a month, or sometimes even less. When she was looking forward to seeing him the most, he would call and say he couldn't make it that weekend, and he hoped she would understand. Then, when Eileen next saw him, he would be distracted, aloof, and uninterested in what was going on in Eileen's life. He did not learn the names of her friends or her teachers, and did not ask about her grades or how she was doing on the soccer team. He was emotionally unavailable to her.

Eileen wanted me to understand that her father was never mean to her. He never said cruel things and he didn't do anything to hurt her on purpose. But he just didn't seem very interested in having kids. This was a big step for Eileen. She saw that her father's reaction was not about her, but about himself. He was not emotionally available for another's person's feelings, even if that other person was his daughter who needed him. When Eileen visited her father on the weekends, she tried to force him to pay attention to her by being affectionate and loving, sitting in his lap and trying to be close. The more she behaved this way the more her father withdrew.

Eileen saw that she had repeated this pattern with the men she had dated, and that her behavior had nothing to do with these men. Certain issues come out only when we are with other people, because it is when we are with others that we might repeat some of the situations we had to deal with when we were younger.

Eileen came to forgive her father for his emotional unavailability. She saw that, so many years after he had divorced her mother, he had never remarried, nor had he stayed with any one woman for any substantial length of time. She said she felt sorry for him for missing out on having love in his life, but said that she believed he really did love her, just wasn't very good at showing it or at being real with other people. She stopped focusing so much on finding the perfect mate, and began to take pleasure in spending time by herself. She had always wanted a partner and had never just let herself be single before.

Eventually, Eileen met a very nice young man, and took her time getting to know him. Rather than exclaiming that she was in love, she told me that he seemed to have many fine qualities, and she was looking forward to getting to know him better. She was delighted by how calm she felt this time around, and how she had no desire to rush things. In turn, as the relationship grew more serious, the man did not make attempts to grow distant or to push her from him – instead, he proved himself capable of a healthy kind of adult intimacy, just as Eileen was.

Eileen had taken the time to learn more about herself and to heal certain aspects of herself that had contributed to her relationships with men. She had changed, and so had the type of man she attracted.

Eileen had a PCS personality, believing that if only she could act the right way, the other person would be better. She thought she had control over this and tried very hard to get the outcome she wanted, all to no avail. She also thought that if she could just be good enough in some way, someone would want a serious relationship with her. Yet, the problem was not that she was not good enough, but that she chose men who did not want to be close, because she thought she wasn't good enough. As always, self-awareness gave her many options that she hadn't had before.

It seems that most people who have survived extreme difficulty in childhood and go on to have successful lives have PCS personalities – they are strong survivors. If you are one of these people, you have many strengths that will see you through any difficulties. I hope my clients can inspire you and remind you of your own strength as you make strides toward knowing your own Abyss and the prison that you constructed when you were younger as a way to deal with pain and fear. You no longer need the confines of this 'beloved prison' to hold you to a false standard – you are capable of so much more.

Exercises

Exercise 1

Karen and John are married. Karen likes to be needed, and has always made fun of John in what looked like a good-natured way so he would look incompetent. She would then "fix" everything. John has had enough. What happened here to John? To the relationship?

Exercise 2

Joe always criticizes Mary, and she is always insecure. Joe sees her insecurity and thinks his problems aren't so bad – at least he isn't begging for love! Mary's therapist told her Joe's criticisms had nothing to do with her, and that trying to please him won't get rid of the criticism. Why not?

Exercise 3

What do you want a partner to do for you? What are you prepared to do for your partner?

Exercise 4

Think of a few instances in which a significant other criticized you or asked you to do something differently. How did you respond? How would you rate the maturity of your response?

Exercise 5

Many people now struggle with intimacy that occurs too early. After a few dates, they often live together and consider the other person a partner. When this does not work out, as it often does not, a major breakup is involved. Many people define a new romantic interest as "nice," but "nice" is not a whole personality. Even with animals, this is inadequate. For example, I had two basset hounds. One, Mabel, was very sweet, compliant, and snuggly, but she was passive-aggressive and sneaky. Our other basset, Bebop, is grumpy, touchy, affectionate on his terms, and completely open and without deviousness.

Think of a person you have gone out with and write a paragraph about what the person was like. Answer the following questions: What is something you liked about the person? What is something this person would get angry or annoyed about? What was the person insecure about? What was something different about the person you liked or disliked? What made the person feel good about himself? How did he handle it when this didn't happen? Think of other questions you should be asking as well, and try to describe a real and full personality.

Chapter 10

The Abyss

Up until now, we have discussed issues that seem separate but are part of a core structure. I have called the issues – which admittedly cause stress and unhappiness in and of themselves – the spokes of the wheel. I used a circular structure to stress the point that these issues, or spokes, are symptoms of a core difficulty. One doesn't come before the others, and none of them exist in isolation. Instead, they are interrelated, and

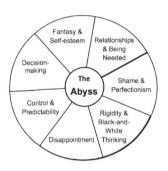

each reflects aspects of the other traits and relates back to the core personality structure.

Assuming you have read the previous chapters and have done the exercises, you will have done some good cognitive work on the spokes themselves, but you have also seen that addressing the spokes, while important, is not the whole picture. For this reason, you have been encouraged and helped to expand your awareness of what is unconscious, to go beneath the surface.

To really modify a personality, you need to become aware of thoughts and feelings that were not conscious before. We have talked, for example, about black–and-white thinking and rigid associations that PCS people make. Recall the people who imagined a whole personality in people who were simply late, or who chose to dye their hair. You will also recall the clients I discussed who thought a little white lie was terrible and felt that they must be brutally honest at all times.

But *why* do people have the specific associations that they do? I will sometimes ask a PCS person why he or she needs to be perfect, and he or she will answer that whenever they were imperfect in the past they were subjected to cruelty or humiliation for not being perfect. This is part of the answer, and a good *historical* one; that is, the answer explains how the behavior or feeling developed and was reinforced in the past. Yet, we are in the present. An historical answer does not address what is in a person's head and heart *now*. That is what this chapter is about.

This chapter lends the book its title. I have called the real and underlying fear PCS people have that manifests in the different spokes the *Abyss*, for a dark, bottomless pit that one fears falling into. The Abyss is not the way you would *like* to think of yourself, but the self-image you fear and try not to know. The spokes of the wheel are designed to help you lose awareness of this feared self-image, to deny it, and to split it into the many different spokes or issues we have discussed. These issues are the price you pay for keeping the Abyss out of awareness.

If only denial worked! If it did, my work would focus on helping people to deny what they feared. The fact is, the issues themselves cause misery for the very person they were intended to protect. When people act "defensive," what they are defending against is their own personal Abyss. It is always easier to see other people's defensiveness than our own, because few people have the courage or awareness to face their own Abyss. Yet, it is the only way to be free from the anxiety-producing spokes and the problems that they carry.

The Abyss, then, is the much-feared self-image that runs counter to the image people pretend they have. It is the hidden self-image that is so feared that PCS people feel they must go to the opposite extreme to deny it. Where does the Abyss come from? Of course, it comes from the past; specifically, it can be rooted in your idea of another person. We often hear people say they are afraid of being like their mother or father. At the time they say this, they do have some awareness of the Abyss, but they then swing to its opposite extreme, in an attempt to over-compensate for these feared aspects of their self-image.

The Abyss, then, can be a dreaded other that forms a hidden part of a person's self-image. A self-image does not have to be accurate, but it nonetheless has a huge influence over the personality. The self-image that represents a dreaded other is defended against by the spokes of the wheel, preventing self-awareness and further emotional growth.

Besides a dreaded other, the Abyss can also be a self-image based on how a person was described or made to feel as a child – a cruel, distorted vision of oneself. As adults, some people still feel awkward, stupid, or unappealing, and go to extremes to avoid this knowledge. When a spoke is tapped, the fear of the Abyss is activated, and the fearful PCS person reacts in one of the ways described here as the PCS traits. The person fleeing from the Abyss unwittingly creates a prison that becomes emotionally stifling.

For many people who have been abused, the Abyss represents one of their parents. They think that if they ever feel angry, they will *become* their abusive mother or father. Less consciously, they feel that they already *are* like that person. While you may feel anger, maybe even rage – just like your parent – you also have values, self-control, and many positive and rational traits. When I say that shining light on your Abyss is the way to heal, I mean that facing feelings you would never act on in a million years enables you to integrate your rage and other traits of your Abyss into your many positive feelings. (See Chapter 5 for a discussion of the integration of feelings). Additionally, you will find that your increased insight makes you less angry or threatened than you were before; as you recognize your own issues, you will find that you do not need to convert them into anger as you have in the past.

When feelings are integrated, they are not pure – they have grown diluted. In this form, rage is much softer than that of a person with no emotional integration. This cannot be stressed enough. This is the central reason why the Abyss and its contents, as well as the meaning of each of the spokes of the wheel, need to come to consciousness.

Maybe your Abyss comes from the way you were made to feel as a child. Maybe you think you are inept or unintelligent. You may even have been a well-treated child who created an Abyss, perhaps feeling guilty for having nice parents. When you face this Abyss, maybe it will become tolerable, even comfortable for you to admit to being unintelligent in certain areas, as we all are. You can then begin to let go of trying to learn *everything*, and simply do what you enjoy and know best. No one can shame you for not knowing something if you already acknowledge that you don't know it, that it is not your strength, and that you don't need to develop intellectually in all possible areas.

In thinking about the issues discussed in this book, it is important to consider the idea of a range of behavior. People all have such a range, and as I often tell my clients, you must look at the range in others to determine whether or not to accept someone into your life. For example, there are people who can be very nice at times, perhaps nicer than most people, but who can also become violent at the other end of their range. This makes it difficult, for example, for battered women to leave abusive men; they talk about how they bring flowers, apologize, and act incredibly nice to them at times. I stress to them that I do not dispute the niceness, but am concerned about the range of behavior the partner displays. I tell them that I would prefer someone who maybe isn't so extremely nice or sensitive at times, but whose other extreme is simply not speaking for a while, or being sarcastic, rather than being abusive.

We are never taught about ranges of behavior, and I have seen a great number of people – smart, high-functioning people – become confused by someone's manipulative conduct because of the "nice" times, and seem to forget or not process the negative end of the range. If, for example, a person is a wonderful friend under happy circumstances and aims for destruction when she is angry, that is not an acceptable friend. We need to know as best as we can what others would do in different circumstances and what their range is.

You need to know your own range as well. I have said that having commonalities with someone who is an abuser, violent, etc., does not make you like them, but this idea of range will clarify this point even further. If you were abused, you know your parent's range, and that range is the problem.

What is your range? What is at the top of your scale, when you are feeling happy and generous? What is at the bottom of your range, when you are angry? Do you just have angry thoughts, if in fact you can acknowledge them? Or, do you sulk, or behave in a passive-aggressive manner? While those behaviors can damage a relationship and can be annoying and even detrimental, they do not make you an abuser or *like* an abuser, and if you are a PCS person with a very safe range, you need not fear looking into your own Abyss.

Some PCS people feel guilty just harboring anger toward their parents, even when there was outright abuse or psychological mistreatment. One reason for this is that most people are not abusive all the time, and even in the worst of homes there are usually some happy memories, periods of truce. Again, this is where the concept of a range is helpful. You deserve the happy memories and they make the unhappy ones easier to bear, but the range of the person who abuses, at the angry end, shows severe lack of control and pure rage. While nothing takes away from the good actions, the negative ones deserve their truth as well, and you need not feel guilty for having angry feelings toward the abuser. A normal person has a normal range, even though these ranges will vary from person to person.

This is also a good time to stress again that while many PCS people – especially those with strong feelings of inadequacy, sadness, and shame – have been abused or otherwise treated badly, not all PCS types come from dysfunctional homes. Some people have kind and loving PCS parents and feel they can never measure up, even though they are loved very much. These people, too, can develop a PCS type of personality, often to the consternation of their parents. Still another scenario is just having normal, affectionate, and competent parents. In this situation there are children who feel guilty because their parents are very nice to them, and develop guilt and the whole PCS constellation. Often, parents are worried and mystified by this and try to help, not knowing how.

It is very hard to raise a child, and, as I always tell people, we're all born to have *some* issues. Children have hostility when they have to do homework, go to bed, or do chores, for example. Some parents are so nice, they do not ever express anger, and the child is left feeling very guilty, overly powerful, aggressive, and ashamed. Parents do not know that they need to teach their children how to manage hostility and that the feeling is normal; these nice, kind parents often have PCS children. I remember when my daughter was seven, she asked me if I ever hated her. I said, "*Yes!* Sometimes you drive me crazy, but I don't feel that way too much." She replied, "Oh, good, Mom, because sometimes I hate you and Dad even though I love you, but if you feel that way, too, maybe I'm not so bad." Having a little hostility mixed with love is the normal human state of affairs, and in a good relationship the love far outweighs what we can call anger or hate, and it is integrated, not pure and not rageful.

There is always a tension in raising children between building competence and supporting self-esteem. Is the way a table is set more important than how a young child feels about herself? Yet, what happens if the child never learns to do things the right way? There is no right answer and, to complicate matters even further, all children are different. A nice, normal parent can tell a child to always do his best, and there is nothing wrong with that. But children cannot evaluate how much something matters and when something is just not worth much effort. I know many adults who developed perfectionistic personalities and carry tremendous guilt for the most minor of activities because they were never taught that some things are just not that important, and certainly the parent never meant for that to happen. Still, a parent who never stresses making an effort or doing your best can end up with a child who never even tries to achieve anything.

Maybe if we didn't have any emotional tension or issues, we would never achieve anything at all. What a lazy child needs to hear is not the same as what an innately PCS child needs to hear. I have met many young adults who were very sad that their mothers never expressed more praise and affection, but they are wonderful young adults. Then there are those who say they had happy lives but can't figure out any direction in life because nothing seems to drive them.

Therefore, you need to look at the range of behavior of those who raised you as well as your own. You need to be honest with yourself about what was difficult for you, what was dysfunctional or abusive, or whether you developed guilt because you sensed your parent as too nice and felt that you were too aggressive inside. While many people come from unfortunate homes with troubled parents, there are many PCS people who have wonderful parents and who at a young age decided that they could never be that good, a feeling that their parents in a million years did not want them to ever have and never even thought of it.

Parents have a range of behavior in reality, but more important is how that range is perceived by their children, and that perception is what develops our personality traits to a great extent. I used to hate when my mother was angry or in a bad mood, but I was not a PCS child. I did not blame myself for my mother's moods and usually knew what caused them. They did not last long and I would feel rather put upon and avoid her until she was in a better one. Later, my own daughter, who had very strong PCS tendencies, clearly felt guilty and needed to ask me if I ever felt negatively toward her. If she had not asked the question, she would have built more and more guilt about her own angry feelings, whether or not she misbehaved.

The point of this digression is that not only must you think in terms of ranges of behavior in evaluating your own childhood and yourself, but you must determine where your own feelings of guilt originate. You must also understand that your own range is what distinguishes you from an abuser.

All of the spokes are symptoms. They were designed to keep you away from the Abyss. But, like all emotional defenses, they cause problems of their own. In today's climate of wanting quick fixes, the spokes or the symptoms are regarded as the problem, and are addressed as problems in their own right. The point is that you fear the Abyss. When you face it, the fear drops away.

You now know what the spokes of the wheel are, and you know that some PCS people, under certain conditions, can develop a panic disorder or clinical depression when their defenses are threatened. Recall the person who could not deal with losing his job because he thought it meant he was stupid. The loss of his job activated the perfectionism and shame spokes and he became clinically depressed. We also discussed a client who developed a severe panic disorder because she could no longer tolerate the career her parents had chosen for her, but felt that a "perfect" child could not go against her parents' wishes.

If the spokes are addressed therapeutically, people like these will never be depressed or panicked for the same reason again. But, if only the depression or panic itself is addressed without regard for the underlying causes, the person will always remain vulnerable to the exact same thing happening again. When you face the Abyss – and by now you know what yours is – you can acknowledge your thoughts and feelings to yourself. You are then in a position to integrate your feelings.

It is very important for you, the PCS reader, to understand that sometimes people with very serious problems can mimic some PCS traits, but they lack the strengths, the self-control, and what we call the ego strength PCS people have. I have had PCS clients with a parent who was a neat freak, even to psychotic proportions, who periodically would explode and abuse the children. This violence unequivocally disqualifies them as having the PCS personality. Certainly, they try to ward off the terror of their internal lives with rigidity and through trying to control everyone else. However, their own loss of control and cruelty means they are *not* PCS personalities, but instead individuals with much more severe issues.

When such people face a real or imagined slight, they do not engage in the self-criticism you might. Instead, they lose touch with reality and respect for morality as they lash out, in an attempt to squash the imposed threat to their very fragile and fragmented sense of self. I knew of a woman who abused her baby because she said he was crying through the night deliberately to bother her. This was *not* a PCS person, regardless of how neat her house might have been. Remember, the spokes of the wheel do not exist in isolation; when a personality contains one or perhaps a few of these spokes, but not the core personality, we do not refer to that personality type as a PCS personality.

Many PCS people fear the Abyss of an internalized abusive parent because they see similarities in themselves. It is essential that you understand that similarities do *not* make you like another person. What does a serial killer who likes to hurt, dominate, and control others, who keeps a neat house and careful records of his heinous crimes, have in common with a kind, efficient, excellent nurse who likes to care for those who need her, and who likes order? The answer is: they have *nothing* important in common. It is the nurse this book is intended for, and people like the nurse. My hope is to help people like the nurse to feel calmer, more self-accepting; to stop worrying about being like someone else who is entirely different; and to stop being terrified of individual traits that do not add up to the same personality as an abusive parent.

This book is not about telling you to beat a pillow and "get in touch" with your anger until you build up to a tantrum. It is about acknowledging your feelings so that you do not live in an anxious and defensive mode, with spokes that undermine every occasion – spokes designed to distract you from your fear of being a way you would never be. Let's look at an example.

Suppose a PCS person is treated unfairly by his boss and accepts this behavior to keep the job. If this PCS person's Abyss is of being abusive and violent like his father, he will actually side with the boss and find excuses for his bad behavior, then find some way to blame himself. A healthy person who is *not* a PCS type might recognize that the boss cannot be reasoned with and not say anything, but will go home and acknowledge to himself or to someone else that he is angry, hates his boss, and wishes the guy would get fired. A strong PCS type whose Abyss causes fear of acknowledging anger, whether to himself or to a trusted and safe loved one, will then deny the anger to himself, and this is very unhealthy.

It's important for you to know that good, kind, normal people sometimes feel envy, greed, spite, and anger. They sometimes have thoughts and feelings that they know better than to act on. Many PCS people do not let themselves even dislike someone for these very reasons, thinking that the thoughts or feelings, *in themselves*, are just as wrong as the behaviors that the thoughts and feelings can lead to for individuals lacking in self-control. Again, those individuals do not have PCS personality structures.

It must be understood that in the PCS personality, negative thoughts and feelings can be acknowledged and processed, rather than denied. Acting on those feelings is very separate from simply owning up to them – an exercise which you can practice privately, or, when you feel comfortable, with a psychotherapist or a trusted loved one.

When I was in college, there was a professor who was much disliked. He would make fun of people in class, write nasty remarks on papers, and do his best to shame and humiliate his students. It was not uncommon for someone to cry in class. Once a group of us were talking at break, noting how the class size had shrunk from about thirty to twelve people, and how we all felt sick before coming to class. A female student said, "I wish something would happen to get rid of him. This is intolerable." We all agreed.

A few days later, we learned that this man had died in an accident. We all looked at each other, and the girl who had made the comment said she felt like she had killed him. The others said that they also felt guilty. I did not feel this way, even though his death was a shock.

I told my classmates that we had done nothing to cause the accident, and that I could not pretend that this had been a good or kind man. I said that I would respect the somberness of the occasion but would not feel guilty or pretend I did not feel relief for having a different professor take over this required class. Another professor did take over, and from that point on, the class became the pleasurable experience it should always have been.

I learned a few years later that this professor's son told a classmate that he had hated his father, and felt guilty because his death had been a relief. It is a tragedy to spend one's life making others miserable, so that one's death causes them to feel this sad mixture of relief and guilt. But the point here is that people who would never do anything seriously wrong have "negative" thoughts and feelings, and that does not make you a bad person – only one who is honest with yourself. Wishing someone were out of your life and feeling relieved when they are is not the same thing as causing harm to them.

People who were abused are afraid of being abusers; this is well known. And it is true that most abusive people were abused themselves. The problem is when you turn it around. Many abused people are so sensitive to the feelings of others they could never abuse anyone. Many of those who have been abused become PCS people. Something bad may have happened to you, but this does not make *you* bad. Having normal anger does not make *you* an abuser. Similarly, missing a day of work does not make you an addict who neglects his family, and telling a little white lie does not make you a con artist or a thief.

You know what your Abyss is. I encourage you to look at it gently, perhaps gradually, respectfully, and as compassionately as you can, so that you don't suffer through so many spokes in your daily life. You can then integrate your feelings, and enter much more fully into self-awareness. You can *feel* angry or frustrated, but you will not *become* the rage, perhaps like someone you have known used to do. You can do this because your anger becomes integrated with all the love and good intention you have ever had in your life. It is not pure, unadulterated rage; it is rage mixed with compassion, humility, empathy, and love, unlike in the explosive person, whose rage is pure. It is when rage is pure that people do very wrong things. This is what it means to shine light on your Abyss. You won't need to be afraid that any detail of commonality with a former abuser will take the good away from you. You will have faced the Abyss and integrated a normal range of human emotion.

Exercises

Exercise 1

Are you afraid of being like someone else, or are you afraid of the way you once felt or were made to feel? Is your Abyss of a dreaded other, or of a distorted image of yourself?

Exercise 2

Think of a couple of associations you have formed and lived by that had their origins in your fear of the Abyss. How did they protect you? What price did you pay for this?

Exercise 3

Were you ever annoyed by a PCS person? Can you understand why he or she acted that way?

Exercise 4

Can you look at some of your issues or spokes and figure out how they protected you from the Abyss?

Exercise 5

Do you still fear the Abyss, even knowing what you now know? If so, can you begin to imagine a more tranquil state?

Chapter 11

Your Authentic Self

I once treated a very wealthy and successful professional woman in her early 40s. "Amy" and her husband, who was also a professional, had three children together. She was used to telling people what to do, and dealt with pressure, a great deal of money, and power in her work life. She said in passing that her husband never told her he loved her, but everything was "wonderful" in their relationship. When I asked if she had ever thought about whether the effect of her childhood or her experience of her parents had any bearing on her choice of marriage partner, she said that she hadn't. Did she ever reflect or meditate on her feelings? "No, never," she said.

Amy had come to me on a friend's recommendation. She had begun to get sweaty hands, would sometimes cry for no apparent reason, and had serious panic attacks. She had been to a psychiatrist who gave her medication, but who told her that there was no cure for her panic disorder. She was frantic. I told her that as she became aware of what her underlying mind was trying to tell her, the panic would ease up.

Amy suffered from PCS traits. She had a brother who was very disturbed, and in his way, the family troublemaker. Although she said her parents and childhood had been "wonderful," it came to light that her father was a very angry man whose behavior bordered on violent. The mother was a kind but passive woman. Amy visited her family several times a year; her father still bullied her mother. Amy decided very early that she would do what she had to to avoid her father's wrath. Given little affection, she would often take care of her depressed mother and try to win her father's approval. An excellent student, as well as popular with her classmates, she felt lonely all the time and often told me that her social life was "all fake," and that she couldn't stand any of the people she interacted with.

Amy told me fairly early in treatment, "Look, I don't want to *control* this. I was already told my panic disorder would never go away, and that's just not good enough. I didn't always have this. Just let me have the bottom line."

"Well, Amy, the bottom line is that there has been pain in your life," I replied. "You survived the pain by being perfect, but without any awareness. You have been unhappy for a long time, and you 'handle' the people in your life like you do your business projects. The very bottom line is that you need to get in touch with your feelings and face them to not have this panic. You are trying to push back thoughts that are trying to come to the surface, and the clash produces the panic attacks." Amy said, "Okay. I have to do that stuff, huh? That's what my friend told me. Is there no other way to get rid of it once and for all?" I told her I didn't know of one. She responded, "Okay, now I know, and I'll do what I have to, but I want you to know I don't like it."

Amy was a true businesswoman in every sense of the word. She remained true to her commitment to our therapeutic work and "tackled" the issues we examined together. She came to see that she married a man much like her father, very cold and troubled. She realized she was desperately unhappy in her marriage and in her work, which was extremely painful to face. After much effort on Amy's part over many months, the panic attacks stopped. She came to see that these attacks were her real thoughts and desires trying to surface. She came to see how sorry she felt for her mother, and that she had thought that being perfect would somehow save her. She talked to her mother about why she remained with her father, and the mother told her that it was indeed very hard, but that she had always been afraid to leave. Amy was able to put limits on her father's behavior at family gatherings, and she and her mother became closer.

Amy did go through a depressed period, as her anxiety had actually covered up the depression she had been afraid to face. She even said to me once, "This depression stinks, but it beats being terrified." When I once told her that the cure for anxiety was depression – meaning that repressed, underground feelings are never happy ones – she called it a "hard sell," which is now a term I use with my clients all the time. Yet, as she said, sadness certainly beats being terrified or panicked.

Though no one likes to feel depressed, clients who have arrived at depression *from* a chronically anxious state are able to acknowledge that in depression they are at last in touch with their true feelings. The process that clients go through might be likened to disillusionment. In Amy's case, her illusion was that her childhood and her husband were both "wonderful." But this is not how she truly felt about them at all. Once this was acknowledged, Amy experienced disillusionment and the accompanying sadness one would expect from the shattering of any illusion.

As we worked through her depression, Amy came to accept that she couldn't control everything. She understood now that her parents' choice to remain together was not her issue but theirs. Her mother went through a very painful divorce from her husband, but enjoyed the new closeness with her daughter. Amy came to see that her business skill was born of wanting to control others and control outcomes, and that this was not really what she wanted to do with her life, although she remained in her career during this time because it was stable and she had other issues to work on.

There came a point where Amy saw that she had been living blindly. She had to mourn this as well and accept that she, like everyone else, had vulnerabilities. Amy eventually combined being a businesswoman with teaching, which worked out well for her. At a business meeting, she had a chance to talk to a man she had always thought was nice. He invited her for drinks and talked about his recent divorce. His story was similar to Amy's, as he saw that he had also been living blindly. Amy began to date him after terminating therapy. She called a few years later to let me know that she was newly married to this wonderful person, was very, very happy, and the panic had never bothered her again.

Amy is a rather extreme example of not living authentically. She felt like a stranger in her own life. If you pretend to be perfect so that you might receive the validation of others, how can you live authentically?

It is really no wonder that our culture produces so many people suffering from PCS or shame-related issues. Excessive emphasis is placed on being better than others, and we call this sense of superiority "self-esteem." We see young children crying hysterically when they do not get an "A" in a subject, and adults judging themselves by how much money they have, the size of their home, their cars, etc. Young people are encouraged to play sports, and they learn quickly how upset coaches and parents become when their team fails to defeat another.

We live in a highly competitive environment. When people apply for jobs and don't get hired, they feel they have done something wrong; there is almost no awareness that other applicants are going through the same experience. We are taught almost from birth to measure ourselves not only by comparing ourselves to others, but by using parameters that are superficial at best, and mean-spirited at worst.

Yet, despite all of these cultural influences, many people are turning to different types of spirituality, whether Eastern or Western, that emphasize self-awareness rather than one-upmanship. Having achieved the success they believed would ward off the Abyss forever, these people found the promise of achievement a hollow one, and still felt something missing in their lives. They learned the hard way that what they *have* is not what they *are*. Many turn to meditation in an effort to find more authenticity, which is good for those it helps.

But another way is to actively and honestly reflect on how you feel, and to do the exercises in this book. Who you are and what you are afraid of being must be acknowledged in order for you to really have choices. As we have seen, the alternative is to anxiously go through each and every interaction with a script of your own, feeling that you must constantly prove something, or more accurately, *disprove* something.

There is an alternative. You can acknowledge your true feelings to yourself and stop living as though you must constantly deny them. You can stop looking to others and to your possessions to tell you who you are, as you constantly struggle against acknowledging your personal Abyss. Instead, you can face your feelings, incorporate them, and have real choices in life. You will not need people to feed a false image or to approve of all of your ideas, and you will be able to be present and aware in your interactions.

Life is not necessarily easy when you are self-aware, but self-awareness is the cure for the pain and anxiety of PCS traits and problems that stem from them. Many people are not aware, and you will be quick to see when others are living defensively. It can be lonely to be more aware, but you will at last be free of having to impress others in order to deny your fears. You will have faced and accepted them as part of being human.

It is a wonderful feeling to be able to admire someone or to be happy for a close friend without making an unfavorable comparison to yourself. You can be grateful for the gifts and strengths you were born with and work on areas that need improvement, or else let them go, and you can see others in the same light. It is incredibly freeing to not have to be perfect, and to just be the person you choose to be, as it is really not possible to evolve without authenticity. You can come to realize that you are meant to be here and have a right to be, and let go of the terrible anxieties that you have always lived with.

When you are honest and authentic with yourself, you have choices about what to share and what not to. When you behave in a people-pleasing way, trying to be perfect when there are things you do not agree with or want to do, you then wonder if people really like you or just the persona. I am not suggesting that you go around telling people off or being cruelly blunt. But if you relate to others by constantly trying to show them how good you are, you are not really living from the heart and letting yourself have full relationships. As we have discussed, this mode of interaction does not make room for the other person's needs.

When you are not authentic with yourself, you don't realize you have choices. You may follow a script you feel someone else has written, which can result in feelings of depression, anxiety, even panic – or you may just develop a chronic sense of unease. Whenever someone else suggests doing something, and you go along with it but have an anxiety attack, it means that a part of you does not want to do it and your unconscious is trying to make you aware of this. You will always have an unconscious, but if you let it play the important role that it is meant to, and listen to it, it will help you to be authentic with yourself.

As you have seen, it is the way we identify with what we have internalized that produces an Abyss. If it remains unconscious, it continues to rule you. Once it is scrutinized, the falseness is seen almost immediately. All of the issues in this book relate back to an unconscious core with a certain pattern. The pattern can manifest in different ways, but lacking self-awareness deprives you of taking pleasure in others and even in yourself.

Much suffering is self-inflicted. It may have had its origins with other people, but it reaches the point where, as a friend once put it, "I can feel miserable all by myself." It is tempting to run from a painful feeling, and yet you have seen how the real cure for this is not to run but to find a way to embrace the feeling with respect, as you gain in understanding.

What is it like to be authentic with yourself? What does it mean? One thing it does *not* mean is that you tell everyone all of your feelings. Neither does it mean that you are never sad or lonely, or that you like every single tendency in your personality. What it does mean is that you are more present.

For example, if you interact with someone who has a trait or talent you enjoy, you can experience genuine admiration without making unfavorable comparisons with yourself; you can simply enjoy the other person. You can even feel gratitude in all its humility – a truly beautiful feeling – when someone does something for you that makes a difference in your life. You can enjoy various activities and interactions without the strain of feeling you are putting on a show and have to convince others (and, of course, yourself) that you are perfect. This lets you be spontaneous and have a good time without having anything to prove. On the job and in your life, you can understand the natural consequences of your actions without beating yourself up and wondering if you are a good person or bad person for some minor incident.

You can also experience the freedom of being wrong or not knowing something, or the humility of saying you're sorry when you make a mistake. You do not need to have overly-simplified views of yourself and others, and do not have to make associations that are false or shallow. You can experience the complexity of just being human, as well as the inconsistencies of yourself and others. You do not have to have so many strict rules and be judgmental of yourself and others, because you know what your Abyss is and you do not project it onto others in a judgmental way. You can have your intuitions, which may be correct or incorrect, but you can have them.

In my eighteen years as a psychotherapist, PCS types of people have always told me at the beginning of therapy how they were unable to understand or read others. They would describe interactions with others to me and have no clue as to what the other person was thinking or feeling. I would understand what the other person's thoughts and feelings had been – it would seem clear to me – and I hadn't even been there! This is a huge benefit of being authentic.

Time and time again, my clients tell me how they can now understand others. Instead of interpreting the behavior of others based on their own, they can understand the associations that others may have. They can see how other people are also afraid of being shamed or embarrassed. For the first time in their lives, they really "see" other people, instead of living in a world that consists of just trying to avoid knowing their own Abyss. My clients are always so happy when they discover that they can really understand others outside of their own tendencies and needs.

While the way out of depression, anxiety, and all the PCS spokes that produce unease is honesty with yourself and self-awareness – in other words, authenticity – I believe that being authentic also means that you fully experience living, though this is not always easy. Many people for the first time see others doing what they used to do – having to be right, having to be the one who gets everything done, who is needed, judging others – and they feel sadness for all the time they have spent doing just that. Other people are excited by their lack of defensiveness and wish to interact more authentically with others, only to realize that there are so many who still suffer from PCS kinds of pain. They feel strongly pressured to follow a script with these people, just like others used to feel with them. Sometimes they feel understandable resentment because, after so much work on oneself, there are still so many people who choose not to do this.

I never heard anyone say that they preferred the anxiety and problems of the PCS state, or that they would give up the wholeness they have, but I have heard clients express deep sadness and loneliness about people wanting to be better than everyone else. This is the trade-off of living authentically. It will not be a given that you find a great number of other people who are also prepared to enter fully into relationships with you, but it is so very meaningful when you do find those capable

of this. It becomes apparent that it is not the quantity of close relationships that matters, but the quality of a few authentic relationships
that can make all the difference in a person's life.

The next step after developing one's own authenticity is to cultivate
empathy and compassion for other people's pain and for those who
have not mustered the courage to make changes. This can be extremely
difficult, and yet, once you have awareness, it is there to stay.

Being authentic will not make your world perfect. Far from it. It
will, however, enable you to be *you*, to see yourself and others and to
care or not care for others, instead of constantly worrying how they feel
about you. Your world will open up tremendously and you will know
that being authentic is a more developed state of mind. And, when
you think about it, what choice is there? You remember how you were
unhappy before, and now you can have tranquility and peace, as well
as more mature relationships. No, they will not be perfect, but they
can be honest, decent and real.

In this book you have read about how many people with PCS traits
have to carry an enormous emotional burden to keep thinking of themselves the way they would like to, in spite of, or because of, the way
they think they really are deep inside. This is the opposite of being
authentic with yourself, and my hope is that this book has helped you
achieve greater awareness, authenticity, and peace, as those really go
together. I wish you all the joys that awareness and authenticity bring,
and I wish you luck and success in your journey toward more emotional
fulfillment.

References

Erikson, E. (1950). *Childhood and Society*. New York: Norton & Company.

Høeg, P. (1993). *Smilla's Sense of Snow*. Trans. T. Nunnally. New York: Delta.

Klein, M. (1975a). Love, Guilt, and Reparation. In R. Money-Kyrle (Ed.), *Envy and Gratitude and Other Works 1921-1945* (pp. 306-343). New York: The Free Press (Original work published 1937).

Klein, M. (1975b). Notes on some schizoid mechanisms. In R. Money-Kyrle (Ed.), *Envy and Gratitude and Other Works 1946-1963* (pp. 1-24). New York: The Free Press (Original work published 1948).

Winnicott, D. (1953). Transitional objects and transitional phenomena. *International Journal of Psychoanalysis*, 340, 89-97.

About the Author

Dr. Aleta Edwards has been a practicing psychotherapist for over twenty years. In addition to her private practice, she has worked with children and adolescents involved in the child welfare system, counseled seniors in a nursing home setting, and treated active-duty military. She has had an interest in shame and perfectionism for many years. She is also a level-two Reiki healer.

Dr. Edwards is married and has one daughter. She is a devoted dog-lover, and has had many loving canines in her life. She lives and works in Tampa, Florida.

Please visit her at her website, her Facebook page, and follow her on Twitter.

- aletaedwards.com

- facebook.com/doctoraleta

- twitter.com/AletaEdwards

Also available from Red Pill Press

Personality-Shaping Through Positive Disintegration

Kazimierz Dabrowski

For psychologist and psychiatrist Kazimierz Dabrowski, personality is not a given – it must be consciously created and developed by the individual. In his second English-language book, Personality-Shaping Through Positive Disintegration, first published in 1967, Dr. Dabrowski presents a comprehensive treatment of personality that is still relevant, perhaps more so today than when it was first written. Here Dabrowski describes personality's individual and universal characteristics, the methods involved in shaping it, and case studies of famous personalities (including Augustine and Michelangelo) demonstrating the empirical and normative nature of personality development.

Grounded in Dabrowski's theory of positive disintegration, Personality-Shaping introduces the concepts at the heart of the theory and at the heart of human potential, creativity, social service, inner conflict, mental illness, and personal growth. Dabrowski's all-embracing perspective is at once a fresh alternative to the one-dimensional theories and trends pervasive in the field of psychology, and a full statement in its own right of all those aspects of human nature too often marginalized, ignored, or denied – a revolutionary and heartfelt product of Dr. Dabrowski's incisive observations and all-embracing vision.

ISBN 978-0692427491

Printed in Great Britain
by Amazon

83313576R00119